THROUGH THE LENS OF IMAN

REFLECTIONS FOR THE SOUL

MUFTI MUHAMMAD TAQI USMANI

TRANSLATION AND NOTES BY ABEER ARAIN

Through the Lens of Imān: Reflections for the Soul

First published in England by
Kube Publishing Ltd,
Markfield Conference Centre,
Ratby Lane, Markfield,
Leicestershire LE67 9SY,
United Kingdom.

Distributed by
Kube Publishing Ltd.
Tel: +44(0)1530 249230
Email: info@kubepublishing.com
www.kubepublishing.com

Cataloguing-in-Publication Data is available from the British Library.

ISBN 978-1-84774-243-8 Hardback
ISBN 978-1-84774-244-5 ebook

Cover design: Amaan Anasari
Typesetting by: LiteBook Prepress Services
Translated by: Abeer Arain
Printed by: Elma Basim, Turkey

Contents

Foreword

In today's world, our modern society is too preoccupied with following western philosophy and values. Social media platforms are readily available for displaying wealth and luxury lifestyles, whether it is genuine or not. Unfortunately, we are surrounded by a never-ending competition for acquiring more wealth and attention. In the midst of these worldly distractions, it has become difficult for Muslims to build a strong connection with Allah ﷻ and the Qur'an. We fall into the trap of *ghaflah* (heedlessness), where people are not concerned whether they are living their daily lives according to the laws of Allah ﷻ and the Sunnah of His Prophet ﷺ. In the Qur'an, Allah ﷻ has mentioned that the temporary life of this world is beautified for the disbelievers and is nothing but amusement and play. For the obedient Muslims, Allah ﷻ has promised an eternal life without sickness, jealousy, or death. They will remain young, and never become old and destitute. There will be everlasting happiness and never-ending joy.

One of the best ways to realign our thoughts and rectify our mistakes is to acquire knowledge from scholars who spend their life teaching the Book of Allah ﷻ. This not only keeps us informed but also strengthens our connection to our *dīn*. In the current times when it is easy to get distracted by the temptations of wealth, fame, and ostentation, we have teachers who are spreading beneficial knowledge of *dīn* without asking for anything in return. One such person is Shaykh Mufti Muhammad Taqi Usmani who is blessed with great knowledge by Allah ﷻ.

Mufti Taqi Usmani belongs to a family of Islamic scholars, and he has authored more than 100 publications on various topics, including Islamic finance, Qur'anic sciences, and exegesis of the Qur'an. His speeches are known for their simple language and uncomplicated symbolizations from everyday life. The anecdotes of his ancestors also impart a strong impression on his audience. Shaykh Usmani's speeches had a tremendous impact on my life as well. Therefore, I decided to compile some of them in a short book as my humble contribution to benefit my Muslim sisters and brothers around the globe.

Through the Lens of Imān is a compilation of Shaykh Usmani's enlightening and thoughtful speeches on various occasions. He delivered the talks in Urdu, and *Alhamdulillah* they are now translated into English to reach a broader audience in the West. This book aims to bring our attention to the common matters of everyday life and relate them to the teachings of the Qur'an and Sunnah.

I would like to thank Shaykh Mufti Taqi Usmani and his team at Darul Uloom, Karachi, Pakistan, for allowing me to translate and publish his work. I would also like to extend my thanks to Brother Haris Ahmad and his editorial staff at Kube Publishing for facilitating the publication of this book.

May Allah ﷻ accept this humble effort from us and make this book a source of *sadaqah jaariyah* (perpetual charity) for us, and I pray that the readers find this book beneficial, āmīn.

Sincerely,
Abeer Arain
Idaho, United States

Time and Trade

وَذَكِّرْ فَإِنَّ الذِّكْرٰى تَنْفَعُ الْمُؤْمِنِيْنَ ﴿٥٥﴾

And remind, for indeed, the reminder benefits the believers. (al-Dhariyat 51: 55)

The above ayah discusses the concept of a 'reminder'. *Fadhakkir* is the word mentioned in the Qur'an for the term reminder, and it comes from *tadhkeer* which has the literal meaning of 'reminding about something that has been forgotten'. It may also mean 'to remind about one's inattentiveness'. The 'reminder' mentioned in the above ayah is about the actual goal for our life. Why are we sent to this world, and what are we actually doing?

We are so consumed in the worldly life that its real meaning seems to have been lost. When we study the life of our Prophet's ﷺ companions, we find that they had a habit of reciting Surah al-Aṣr before adjourning their gatherings.

وَالْعَصْرِ ﴿١﴾ إِنَّ الْإِنْسَانَ لَفِيْ خُسْرٍ ﴿٢﴾ إِلَّا الَّذِيْنَ اٰمَنُوْا وَعَمِلُوا
الصّٰلِحٰتِ وَتَوَاصَوْا بِالْحَقِّ ﴿٠﴾ وَتَوَاصَوْا بِالصَّبْرِ ﴿٣﴾

(I swear) by the Time, indeed man is in a state of loss, except those who believed and did righteous deeds exhorted each other to follow truth and exhorted each other to observe patience. (al-Aṣr 103: 1-3)

What was their purpose of reciting Surah al-Aṣr? It is because in Surah al-Aṣr, Allah ﷻ reminds us of the designated time we are given in this world in a very powerful way, and when Allah ﷻ reminds us that as humans we are at a loss, it means that He demands our immediate attention. We are at a major loss unless we remain steadfast, perform good deeds, and encourage others to be patient and righteous. That is because every human being comes into this world with a limited time, and only Allah ﷻ knows how much time has been allotted to each of us. The departure from this world is a universal truth accepted by everyone who walks on this earth, irrespective of their beliefs. Nobody denies the certainty of death.

The time given to us is like a bag of trading goods. Everyone arrives in this world with ample stock. The purpose is to trade our goods in a way so that we can benefit from Allah's approval and blessings by being granted *Jannah* (happiness and peace forever). If a trade is done according to the rules of Allah ﷻ, we depart with a bag containing a much larger profit. On the contrary, a careless deal may not bring any benefit but may lead to negative revenue.

My father, Mufti Muhammad Shafi (may Allah ﷻ grant him *Jannah*) once narrated an interesting story of a nawab (ruler) of Bengal in the olden times.[1] The nawab

1. Shaykh Usmani's father, Mufti Muhammad Shafi (1897 – 1976) was a prominent scholar from the Indian Subcontinent (and later migrated to Pakistan). He authored Ma'ariful Qur'an, one of the most widely read commentaries on the Holy Book. In 1951, he founded

lived a prosperous life, but unfortunately, he died untimely. Upon his departure from this world, his son and daughter inherited his wealth. The nawab's son once ignited a matchstick and loved the sound and smell of this process. He relished it so much that bundles of matchsticks were ordered. He developed a habit of igniting them day and night. On the other hand, the nawab's daughter visited the market one day and enjoyed the sound of the tearing of some fabric. She bought an entire stock of cloth from the stalls and began tearing up the fabrics for mere enjoyment. The two siblings spent a lot of their time pursuing their respective hobbies. Eventually, a time came when their assets were exhausted. The financial situation turned so dire that the siblings began begging in the same market where they used to invest. Hence, the market was called Begum Bazaar (i.e., Begum, nawab's daughter). The siblings spent their entire wealth seeking pleasure for their senses (nose and ears). This story sounds absurd and funny at the same time. It is hard for us to believe these two adults spent their inherited wealth on such futile activities. Let's relate this story to our lives and how we spend time in this world. Our reality is not much different from that of the nawab's children. Allah ﷻ gave us a bag of trading goods (time), so that we use it carefully and strive to attain the best life in the Hereafter. Unfortunately, we waste much of our merchandise by committing sins, such as listening

---

Darul Uloom in Karachi, Pakistan, which remains one of the most prominent madrasahs in South Asia to this day. The story of the nawab of Bengal is therefore rooted in the Indian Subcontinent, as Mufti Shafi was from the Indo-Pak subcontinent area.

to music, backbiting, having vulgar conversations, wasting time, and lying. We waste money by watching movies, which in turn contain prohibited scenes. In fact, we are in a deeper mental obscurity than the nawab's children because their wealth was the inherited money that belongs to this temporary world. However, our treasure is for the Ākhirah, which is the everlasting and ultimate abode.

We are given our tongue to practise good deeds, such as *dhikr*, reciting the Qur'an, and spreading kindness with our words. But we exploit the gift by backbiting, lying, and indulging in useless conversations. This is the real 'waste' that Allah ﷻ has mentioned in Surah al-Aṣr.

Allah ﷻ has not only given us the trading goods (the time in this world) but also provided us with an enlightening handbook in the form of the Qur'an. He has given us five mandatory prayers as a reminder that any one of them can be the last one. Of course, we are allowed to enjoy our life and attain comforts, but getting lost in the spirals of heedlessness and worldly matters pretermitting the Ākhirah is where things can work against us. This is when a person starts squandering precious goods in the bag of time.

Another reality is that we do not know when our bags will be emptied. With each passing year, it is becoming insubstantial. We depart from this world as soon as we disburse our last commodity. No one, except Allah ﷻ, knows when a person's time will end in this provisional world. Life is unpredictable. Unfortunately, sudden death, such as through road accidents, is common nowadays. Terminal illnesses and fatal diseases are diagnosed frequently, some of which did not previously exist. Our time is one of the most invaluable treasures given to us by Allah ﷻ, and the soul realizes its worth soon after it departs the body, as declared in the following verse:

وَاَنْفِقُوْا مِنْ مَّا رَزَقْنٰكُمْ مِّنْ قَبْلِ اَنْ يَّاْتِيَ اَحَدَكُمُ الْمَوْتُ فَيَقُوْلَ رَبِّ
لَوْلَآ اَخَّرْتَنِيْٓ اِلٰٓى اَجَلٍ قَرِيْبٍۙ فَاَصَّدَّقَ وَاَكُنْ مِّنَ الصّٰلِحِيْنَ ۝١٠

***And spend [in the way of Allah] from what We have provided you before death approaches one of you and he says, "My Lord if only You would delay me for a brief term so I would give charity and be of the righteous."* (*al-Munāfiqun 63: 10*)**

Allah ﷻ has given us a stockpile of precious time for this world, and there will be no dispensation when the Angel of Death appears, and the time is over. That is the real loss.

Let's spend our time the way our Creator has instructed, by following the Sunnah of our Prophet ﷺ and the *dhikr* of Allah ﷻ. And let's not just limit it to ourselves. Let's aim to involve our family members, friends, and the people of our community in this venture. Let's remind ourselves and our loved ones about the irreplaceable asset of time. These reminders are critical because the company of good people who remember Allah

ﷻ brings us closer to Our Creator. On the contrary, wasting time with the ones living in *ghaflah* with no rumination of the Ākhirah will make us forget about our prime goal as well. Allah ﷻ has mentioned in the Qur'an:

وَمَا خَلَقْتُ الْجِنَّ وَالْإِنْسَ إِلَّا لِيَعْبُدُوْنِ ﴿٥٦﴾

***I did not create the jinns and the human beings except for the purpose that they should worship Me.* (*al- Dhariyat 51: 56*)**

So, our life goal should be to worship Allah ﷻ, and everything else is secondary. Unfortunately, we inadvertently neglect our thoughts, energy, and time in worldly life. *Alhamdulillah*, we observe our mandatory prayers, fast during Ramadan, and recite the Qur'an regularly. But what about the rest of the day? Where are the remaining hours exhausted on? Do we think about Our Creator, *Jannah*, or *Jahannam*? The choice is ours whether we make our life an embodiment of the *dhikr* of Allah ﷻ or waste it with heedlessness. We can nourish our souls with the remembrance of Allah ﷻ in our daily routines, such as when we eat, spend time with loved ones, during chores, and while we travel. How often do we think about Allah ﷻ? Is our mind too engrossed with the yearning for preeminence, affluency, and exorbitant designation? With a little effort, such as memorizing the daily supplications, following the Sunnah, and protecting ourselves from the state of *ghaflah*, we can direct our tunneled focus towards life in the Hereafter. May Allah ﷻ make our tongue moist with constant du'ā', *dhikr*, and *shukr*.

Five before Five

"Take advantage of five before five: your youth before your old age, your health before your sickness, your wealth before your poverty, your free time before your preoccupation, and your life before your death." (Shu'ab al-Iman 9767)

In the above-mentioned Hadith, the Prophet ﷺ is telling us about the five treasures of this life. He ﷺ is instructing us to take advantage of these five matters before losing them and that includes this life itself, our health, wealth, free time, and the time of youth. As long as we are alive, we have the opportunity to spend this time wisely, and avoid regret in the Ākhirah.

First, take advantage of health before sickness.[2] Suffering from an illness and not being able to do activities in daily life can be difficult and challenging. For a believer, a sickness of any kind is a trial. It elevates our rank. Forbearing at the time of sickness is like being under the pouring rain of Allah's mercy. Of course, we do not pray for illness, but we must always ask for good health and contentment from Allah ﷻ. We appreciate the value of sound health when we are weak and unwell. When our body is healthy, we have the opportunity to take the utmost advantage of it. We can pray as much as we want, give charity, keep voluntary fasts, and

2. Here, the respected Shaykh is not following the exact sequence of the Hadith and mentioning health first.

perform any kind of virtuous acts. Unfortunately, many of us think that our good health is going to last perpetually, and we may earn good deeds at an older age. But the truth is that sickness can arrive at any time and does not usually give any opportunity to perform good deeds.

At the time of illness, we take the necessary steps to regain our health. It helps us focus on relevant matters in life, which are also beneficial for the Ākhirah. We start to implement the acts of ʿibādah that Allah ﷻ has given to the sick. For example, if we cannot pray ṣalāh while standing, we can pray sitting; if we cannot pray sitting, we can lie on the bed. If we cannot perform wuḍū' using water, we can do *tayammum* (dry ablution using the Sunnah technique with clean soil or a rock). Sickness brings us closer to the practise of supplication and strengthens our bond with Allah ﷻ. From history, we learned the stories of some great scholars who asked Allah ﷻ for recovery from their illness, and once recuperated, they spent the rest of their lives spreading knowledge of the Qur'an by teaching it to others. Thus, our time of prosperity provides a golden opportunity to earn as many good deeds as possible.

Second, take advantage of youth before getting to old age. The youthful years are full of strength and energy. One is able to perform longer ʿIbādah, and other good deeds requiring physical endurance. ʿibādah in the time of youth is the Sunnah of Allah's prophets. Compared to the time of youth, older age accompanies frailty, weaker bones, and many chronic diseases. People typically become cautious of committing sins as they get older.

Even the most deviant ones become religious. They feel concerned about approaching death and pray as much as possible to add good deeds to their account. However, the strength is gone, and the body is much weaker. That is why the time of youth is important. The zeal and energy of youth is to be spent in the path of Allah ﷻ.

The third point in the Hadith is about taking advantage of affluency before poverty. Our monetary state of affairs does not stay the same forever (may Allah ﷻ protect us from destitution). It is Allah's decree who He blesses with wealth and for how long. There are people in society who lose their entire wealth when their business goes bankrupt. The wealth that is wasted in useless activities, such as futile purchasing of items that are not needed, haram excursions, and not paying zakat, metaphorically becomes a tight rope around the neck. This rope becomes the cause of Allah's wrath, and once pulled, the proud person falls to the ground, asking people for food after being afflicted with poverty. In one Hadith, the Prophet ﷺ said, "The son of Adam boasts: My wealth! My wealth! O Son of Adam, have you truly earned any wealth but what you ate and consumed, or clothes put on and wore out, or spent in charity so it remained?" (Ṣaḥīḥ Muslim 2958)

"This wealth is sweet (alluring); whoever earns it lawfully and spends it rightfully, then what excellent help it is!" (Ṣaḥīḥ al-Bukhari 6441)

The fourth point in the above-mentioned Hadith is about appreciating our free time before getting occupied. A person is often busy in the daily chores of life.

However, there are a few hours each day that provide some spare time to all of us. One must recognize the significance of these hours and use them for the betterment of his Ākhirah. This time can be spent in reciting the *Qur'an*, sending salawat on the Prophet ﷺ, giving *sadaqah*, and so on. The time we have is like a jewel and once gone, we get no feasibility to do good deeds, such as recite the Qur'an or do the *dhikr* of Allah ﷻ. One way to benefit our time is to plan the day. Generally, children learn these basic concepts from an early age. They observe their parents who are their role models when it comes to time management. Ibn Hajar (a famous scholar, known for his commentary on Ṣaḥīḥ al-Bukhari) had an excellent technique of utilizing his hours. During his time, people used wooden pens and inkpots for writing. The pen had to be fine-tuned every so often and Ibn Hajar used to sharpen his pen while doing the *dhikr* of Allah ﷻ (*SubhanAllah, Alhamdulillah, Allāhu Akbar*). We must realize that our time is like a burning candle that is melting every minute.

The final point is about acknowledging our time in this world before our final departure. Death is certain and is the biggest reality of our life. There is no objection regarding this in any religion. Even an atheist believes in the occurrence of death. As Muslims, we know that our book of deeds gets closed after death and there is no way we can return to pray, fast, do *dhikr*, or any other acts of worship. We will not be able to return to the *dunya*. The door of sending good deeds forward is now shut. The only three benefits that one continues to receive even after our demise include supplications from the righteous descendants who prays for the deceased parent, *sadaqah jariyaah*, and the knowledge of the deceased that he passed on to benefit others. But the deceased himself will not be able to say *istighfar* for his sins, nor be able to say *Alhamdulillah* for the number of days he was given in this world. That is why the Prophet ﷺ forbade us to wish for death, as death closes the door of actions and ways to earn *Jannah*.

It is mentioned in the Qur'an that the deceased will regret the time wasted in life and will plead to Allah ﷻ to send him back so he could give more *sadaqah*. It will be an eternal regret.

وَاَنْفِقُوْا مِنْ مَّا رَزَقْنٰكُمْ مِّنْ قَبْلِ اَنْ يَّاْتِيَ اَحَدَكُمُ الْمَوْتُ فَيَقُوْلَ رَبِّ
لَوْلَآ اَخَّرْتَنِيْٓ اِلٰٓى اَجَلٍ قَرِيْبٍۙ فَاَصَّدَّقَ وَاَكُنْ مِّنَ الصّٰلِحِيْنَ ﴿١٠﴾

"And spend out of what We have given to you before death overtakes one of you and he says, "My Lord, would you not give me respite to a near term, so that I should pay Sadaqah (alms) and become one of the righteous?" (al-Munāfiqun 63: 10)

Therefore, we must spend every minute of this life with consciousness, for eternal success in the Ākhirah. This life is a blessing from Allah ﷻ. It has difficulties and trials, but we are also given opportunities to choose the right path. Allah ﷻ has given us enough time to take advantage and follow the guidelines. When one withstands the trials and remains steadfast on the right path, he gets included in the list of *as'haabul ma'imanah* (the people of the right).[3] Those are the righteous servants of Allah ﷻ who will be given the eternal abode of peace and tranquility.

May Allah ﷻ guide us in spending our time, our health, our youth, and this life in obeying Him and following the Sunnah of the Prophet ﷺ, āmīn.

---

3. Shaykh is referencing the ayah from *Surah al-Wa'qiah* where Allah ﷻ has mentioned the three categories of people in the Ākhirah and the best category is of the people who will be given their book of deeds in their right hand. They have been regarded as the lucky ones in the Qur'an. Allah ﷻ says, "*As for the People of the Right, how (lucky) are the People of the Right!*" (*al-Waqi'ah 56: 8*)

Backbiting

In today's contemporary world, *Alhamdulillah,* we can fulfill the basic obligations to the Almighty, such as praying *ṣalāh* on time, keeping all fasts during Ramadan, and giving *zakat*. However, the biggest concern we encounter is submitting to the wishes of our *nafs* (the inner self). Every human has two major enemies: one is *Iblīs* (*shaytaan*), and the other is our *nafs*. They both push us towards sins, the obvious, and the hidden ones. The obvious ones include robbery, consuming alcohol, looking at haram, lying, backbiting, having haram relationships, and so on. The hidden sins are inside us, in the form of jealousy, pride, ostentation, love of acquiring inexhaustible wealth and fame.

Abu Hurayrah narrated that the Prophet ﷺ was asked, "O Messenger of Allah ﷺ, what is backbiting?" He ﷺ replied, "It is saying something about your brother which he would dislike." He was asked again, "Tell me how the matter stands if what I say about my brother is true." He ﷺ said, "If what you say of him is true, it is backbiting, and if what you say of him is not true, it is slandering." (Sunan Abi Dawud 4874)

One of the most prevalent sins in our society is called *gheebah* (backbiting). It is also known in our society as gossiping, which is to talk about a matter related to a Muslim brother or sister in a way that if it was said in their presence, they would feel distressed. We all know that backbiting is a major sin, yet we are fully involved in it. Backbiting or gossiping has become so customary that none of our gatherings are free from it. We discuss politicians, television personalities, and even the deceased without realizing that we are involved in *gheebah.*

The Prophet ﷺ once said to Abu Dharr raḍiyallāhu 'anhu: "O Abu Dharr! Beware of backbiting, for backbiting is worse than *zina* (adultery)." Abu Dharr said: "Why is that so, O Messenger of Allah ﷻ?" He ﷺ replied: "That is because when a man commits *zina* and then repents to Allah ﷻ, Allah ﷻ accepts his repentance. However, backbiting is not forgiven until forgiven by its victim." (Shu'ab al-Imān 6229)

In the Qur'an, Allah ﷻ has strictly forbidden us from getting involved in major sins such as fornication, alcohol consumption, and theft. However, He mentioned stern warnings along with punishments on some evil actions, such as *riba* (interest), committing murder, and *gheebah* (backbiting).[4] *Riba* is equivalent to fighting a war against Allah ﷻ and the Prophet ﷺ. Furthermore, murdering someone innocent brings the wrath of Allah ﷻ and severe punishment in the Ākhirah. The third sin is *gheebah*, which has been regarded as comparable to ingesting the flesh of your dead brother (*al-Hujurat* 49: 12). Imagine your brother's dead body in front of you and

4. These evil actions bring unrest to society and harm the unity of the ummah. Today, we unfortunately have deep-rooted corruption and immorality in Muslim societies because of widespread usury, innocent killing, and backbiting.

you start cutting it and eating his flesh. This is how bad *gheebah* is, *astaghfirullāh*.

يَاَيُّهَا الَّذِيْنَ اٰمَنُوا اجْتَنِبُوْا كَثِيْرًا مِّنَ الظَّنِّ اِنَّ بَعْضَ الظَّنِّ
اِثْمٌ وَّلَا تَجَسَّسُوْا وَلَا يَغْتَبْ بَّعْضُكُمْ بَعْضًا اَيُحِبُّ اَحَدُكُمْ اَنْ
يَّاْكُلَ لَحْمَ اَخِيْهِ مَيْتًا فَكَرِهْتُمُوْهُ وَاتَّقُوا اللّٰهَ اِنَّ اللّٰهَ تَوَّابٌ
رَّحِيْمٌ ﴿١٢﴾

***O you who have believed, avoid much [negative] assumption. Indeed, some assumption is sin. And do not spy or backbite each other. Would one of you like to eat the flesh of his brother when dead? You would detest it. And fear Allah; indeed, Allah is Accepting of repentance and Merciful.* (*al-Hujurat 49: 12*)**

Often, we hear people say, "I'm not doing *gheebah* because I can say this even in his or her presence", but be aware that this does not wipe away the sin of *gheebah*. Instead, it shows that the person is committing a sin and is boastful about it. Now let's do a self-assessment on our conversations with other people. Do we discuss those who are absent and point out their flaws?

The gatherings of our Prophet's ﷺ companions were free from mockery, backbiting, and slandering. The Prophet ﷺ taught them in a way that their meetings were enjoyable yet free from the disobedience of Allah ﷻ. If anyone's name was mentioned, it was to point out the good in that person.

The Prophet ﷺ once asked his companions,[5] "Who is *muflis* (indigent)?" They said, "Someone who has no money". The Prophet ﷺ replied, "*Muflis* is not the one lacking wealth, but he is someone who will stand in front of Allah ﷻ with a bag full of good deeds (prayers, *dhikr*, fasting, *tahajjud, Umrah, Hajj, Zakat*, etc.), but when his account of deeds will be opened, a crowd will gather around him. Some will recall the *gheebah* he did about them, others will highlight slanders and cheatings he enjoyed in the world (i.e., borrowing someone's money and never returning it). As a result, the crowd will be given his good deeds as compensation. Some will take the deeds from his prayers, while others will get the deeds that he had earned from fasting, *zakat*, etc. Finally, the *muflis* will be left empty-handed with no good deeds. If there are still some people waiting to get their compensation, their bad deeds will be added to the *muflis's* account (Ṣaḥīḥ Muslim 2581). Our Prophet ﷺ regarded this as the true poverty. May Allah ﷻ protect us from such a situation in the Ākhirah, āmīn.

Unfortunately, backbiting is also common in our religious gatherings. Someone who belongs to a different sect becomes the topic of discussion, and we perceive it as if we own the right to criticize that person. As a result, such conversations spread division and hatred amongst Muslims.

---

5. Here, the respected shaykh is describing the *mafhoom* or the congruent meaning of the Hadith and not the exact words.

In order to have healthier gatherings[6], we must be mindful of *gheebah*, and stop others from doing it. In addition, we must protect ourselves by reciting the du'ā' taught to us by the Prophet ﷺ. This du'ā' is from *Surah al-Saffat*:

سُبْحٰنَ رَبِّكَ رَبِّ الْعِزَّةِ عَمَّا يَصِفُوْنَ ﴿١٨٠﴾ وَسَلٰمٌ عَلَي
الْمُرْسَلِيْنَ ﴿١٨١﴾ وَالْحَمْدُ لِلّٰهِ رَبِّ الْعٰلَمِيْنَ ﴿١٨٢﴾

Glory to thy Lord, the Lord of Honour and Power! (He is free) from what they ascribe (to Him)! and Peace on the Messengers! and praise to Allah, the Lord, and Cherisher of the Worlds.
(Al-Saffat 37: 180-182)

---

6. The gatherings that follow the guidelines of the *Sunnah* and the way of Prophet's ﷺ companions.

Overspending

There are wrongdoings that we are aware of and feel remorseful about, such as lying, backbiting, and so on. However, there are matters which are easily disregarded because of our ignorance, and lack of knowledge about their harm. Metaphorically, it is like an individual suffering from a disease, but he is unaware of his illness and therefore, does not seek medical help. As a result, the disease strengthens its roots, eventually taking over the body. One such disease in our society is called *israaf*, also known as squandering or overspending, and it is one of the biggest sins. Allah ﷻ mentions in the Qur'an:

إِنَّ الْمُبَذِّرِيْنَ كَانُوْٓا إِخْوَانَ الشَّيٰطِيْنِ

Surely squanderers are brothers of Shaitan (Bani Isra'il 17: 27)

وَكُلُوْا وَاشْرَبُوْا وَلَا تُسْرِفُوْا

Eat and drink but do not be excessive (i.e., do not go beyond bounds) (Al-A'rāf 7: 31)

The Prophet ﷺ refrained his ummah from wasting money and said, "Allah ﷻ does not like for you to waste wealth'.

There are three major forms of *israaf*. The first form is spending money on utterly forbidden and unlawful activities like watching haram movies, buying alcohol, or eating forbidden food. It is the worst form because it not only wastes the blessing (the wealth given by Allah ﷻ) but also adds sins to our account. The second form is wasting money on something that is not *haram* but is not a necessity. The third and most common form of *israaf* in our society is the mere dissipation of wealth. By wealth, we do not include monetary capital or cash. The food we have and the amount of water we are given are also included in this wealth.

One of the most distinguished scholars, Mawlana Ashraf Ali Thanvi (may Allah ﷻ grant him *Jannah*) once mentioned, "Spending money on a luxury that you are able to afford, and planning on using is not *israaf*, as long as you intend on not showing it off." Wearing higher quality clothing is not *israaf*. In fact, we should dress according to our financial situation. However, if the intent is to make one look superior to others, then the same expenditure becomes *haram*. Therefore, when buying something, question yourself: are you fulfilling your needs, or do you want to flaunt it to show other people? Is your purchase going to harm your Ākhirah or is it going to be beneficial for it?

The Prophet ﷺ once asked his companion, Sa'd, who was performing wuḍū' (ablution) "What is this extravagance?" Sa'd said, "Is there extravagance with water in wuḍū'?" The Prophet ﷺ replied, "Yes, even if you were on the banks of a flowing river." (Musnad Ahmad 7065)

Water is a blessing and is essential for life on earth. The water we utilize for our needs comes from glaciers, oceans, and rivers. If Allah ﷻ decides to put all the water on this planet in one place and leave it to us to fetch it, then the water would become an extremely valuable entity. Do you think we would be able to go to the oceans and bring water individually? Likely not. Allah ﷻ taught us to design the water system in our cities. Unfortunately, what we observe in our society is only the waste of this huge blessing. Let's take the example of performing wuḍū'.

It is narrated by Jabir ibn Abdullah that the Prophet ﷺ used to take bath with a *sa'* (of water) and perform ablution with a *mudd* of water. (Sunan Abi Dawud 93).

If there is a shortage of water, we would still manage to do wuḍū'. But with access to unlimited water, we tend to use more than we should. The Prophet ﷺ used to perform wuḍū' with one *mudd* of water, which is equal to about 0.54 liters.

This is not limited to just water. We must take care of every blessing given to us by Allah ﷻ. Unfortunately, wasting resources is common in our society. We waste our meals during wedding ceremonies and other gatherings. This is because we have limited our *dīn* to *ṣalāh* and fasting and have forgotten to apply the *Sunnah* of our Prophet ﷺ to all aspects of our daily life. Sadly, *israaf* is not considered a transgression in our society anymore.

Whatever possessions we have are a blessing from Almighty Allah ﷻ, and we must be mindful of their use. When eating your meal, remind yourself that it is a great blessing that you otherwise would not have been able to attain on your own. Rather than overeating, one can save it for later or for someone else. When serving our guests, we must allow them to choose how much they would like to eat to avoid the wasting of excess food.[7]

My father (Mufti Muhammad Shafi) once dined with Mawlana Asghar Hussain, a prominent scholar of his time (may Allah ﷻ grant him *Jannah*). When the dinner was over, my father took the tablecloth outside to dust away the leftover food particles. Mawlana asked him not to brush off the tablecloth. He asked my father to bring it back to him. He commented, "Do you know that cleaning the tablecloth is an art?" My father was surprised upon hearing this and asked, "How can a minor thing like cleaning a tablecloth be an art?" Mawlana then splendidly elucidated the concept of recycling. He replied, "Yes, it is an art. You see these leftover bones; they are to be kept in one corner outside the house as the dogs come there to eat. The discarded meat parts are for another corner because the cat sits there. Leftover bread is kept on the rooftop for the crows. The remaining particles are for the ants, and I keep them aside so they can find them. The purpose of this entire process is not to waste anything." *SubhanAllah*. May Allah ﷻ protect us from *israaf* and guide us to spend our money on the causes that please Him.

7. The Shaykh was telling a story about a scholar who attended a dinner party. The host was serving too much food on the guest's plates. The scholar ate a little from his plate and then returned it to the host, asking him to finish it. This was his way of teaching a lesson about the wastefulness of food, which is widespread in our society.

The Love of Wealth

وَتُحِبُّونَ الْمَالَ حُبًّا جَمًّا ﴿٢٠﴾

And you love wealth with immense love.
(*al-Fajr 89: 20*)

Having wealth and luxurious assets is not impermissible in Islam, as long as one earns it through *halal* means. What is debarred is the attachment towards wealth and an obsession to earn more of it, so much so that the distinction between *haram* and *halal* is obliterated. As a result, earning money becomes the centripetal force in one's life. It must be noted that Allah ﷻ does not forbid us to make money or to save it. However, He dislikes that His servant is always busy thinking about making money. A scholar once said, *"Live in this world, but don't be a seeker of this world."* We should use this world to fulfill our needs[8] but not fill our hearts with the love of this world. If we do, we may spend life only seeking worldly desires and fortune.

How do we detach the love of wealth from our hearts? First, we must remember that the property we own and the income we earn is not going to last forever. We must also not forget that the moment our eyes close

8. Fulfil our needs by only buying what is needed, and avoiding everything that is mere a want, an impulse buy, and not a need.

after death, all our wealth will be inherited. Nothing will belong to us.

Anas raḍiyallāhu 'anhu reported that the Messenger of Allah ﷺ said: "Three (things) follow the deceased: members of his family, his property, and his deeds. Two of them return; and one remains with him. The people and his wealth return; his deeds remain with him" (Riyad as-Salihin 460).

The '*property*' mentioned in the above Hadith includes the deceased's shroud and the gurney, which is used to transport his body. Once inside the grave, the stretcher is gone too, and the shroud eventually decomposes. After some time, the family members and relatives also leave the graveyard. The deceased is left lying in the grave only with his deeds. The love of wealth is of no benefit to the one who is dead. It is only the deeds that can either turn the grave into a garden of heaven or the oven of fire. Therefore, it is important to constantly remind yourself that wealth is temporary, but the account of deeds is permanent.

Abu Mut'arrif narrated that he once came to the Prophet ﷺ while he was reciting the verse, "Competition for wealth diverts you." (*al-Takathur* 102:1). The Prophet ﷺ said, "The son of Adam boasts: My wealth! My wealth! O Son of Adam, have you truly earned any wealth but what you ate and consumed, or put on and wore out, or spent in charity so it remained?" (Muslim 2958)

The above hadith summarizes the reality of our assets. We spend our wealth on food and clothes, but it only becomes everlasting when we give it as charity for the sake of Allah ﷻ. This wealth will benefit us in the *Ākhirah* where there will not be any other source of earning.[9]

In *Surah al-Humazah*, Allah ﷻ says:

الَّذِيْ جَمَعَ مَالًا وَّ عَدَّدَهٗ ﴿٢﴾

Who accumulates wealth and counts it
(*al-Humazah 104: 2*)

There is a fascinating story from the archaic times about a wealthy man who owned a huge fortune in the form of gold and silver, and he collected it in a large vault near his home. It was his routine to walk through the site and admire the amount of wealth he had accumulated. His hunger for the mountains of gold and silver coins was endless. One day, he accidentally locked himself in the vault. It turned out that he was the only one who knew how to unlock the door. As a result, the wealthy man got trapped alongside his possessions. Consequently, he died

---

9. The investment that we do for the *Ākhirah*, in the form of *sadaqah*, is the only wealth that remains forever. It gets transformed into the currency of rewards and gets saved in the eternal bank of our good deeds. The significance of this currency is highlighted in a Hadith narrated by Tirmidhi, on the authority of Abu Maisarah, who reported from Aishah that once they slaughtered a sheep and gave its meat in charity. When the charity was done, the Prophet ﷺ asked Aishah raḍiyallāhu 'anhā, "What remains of it?" Aishah raḍiyallāhu 'anhā said, "Nothing remains but its shoulder." The Prophet ﷺ said, "All of it remains except the shoulder." (Tirmidhi 2470).

inside the vault with his enormous wealth. In today's society, some people have secret bank accounts in different countries. After they depart from this world, their assets remain in these accounts, never to be found by anyone.

It is narrated by Sa'd bin Abi Waqas that the Prophet ﷺ said, "You will be rewarded for whatever you spend for Allah's sake, even if it were a morsel which you put in your wife's mouth." (Ṣaḥīḥ al-Bukhari 56)

Islam is a *dīn* of balance, and the above Hadith highlights the rights of our wealth. When Allah ﷻ blesses us with substantial prosperity, we are instructed to spend on food and not deprive our body of nourishment. Likewise, proper clothing is important as it is our body's right to be clothed with good quality garments. Of course, we should dress according to our financial status and budget and not show off.

The Prophet ﷺ said, "If Allah ﷻ has given you wealth, let the traces of His blessings and generosity be seen upon you." (Sunan Abi Dawud 406)

Also, it must be noted that giving money as *sadaqah* does not mean that an individual must donate all his money to charity and not leave anything for their heirs. This would be an extreme act, not liked by Allah ﷻ as mentioned by our Prophet ﷺ when he established the boundaries for *sadaqah*:

Once Saad Ibn Abi Waqas fell ill, the Prophet ﷺ visited him. Saad told the Prophet ﷺ, "O Messenger of Allah, I have a great deal of wealth and only one daughter to inherit from me. Shall I bequeath two-thirds of my wealth in charity?" "No" the Prophet ﷺ replied. Saad asked, "How about half?" "No", the Prophet ﷺ answered. Saad then asked, "One-third?" The Prophet ﷺ said, "One-third, and one third is a plenty." He then gave him a piece of advice and told him, "To leave your heirs rich is better than leaving them poor and asking people for help." (Sunan Ibn Majah 2708)

Once, a man in the time of the Prophet ﷺ lived a poverty-stricken life. He asked the Prophet ﷺ to pray for him to get wealth. Looking at his misery, the Prophet ﷺ prayed for him, and soon the poor man began accumulating wealth, and became the owner of livestock. During that time, wealth was measured by the size of livestock. The man became deeply immersed in the herding of his goats. Shortly after, the number of animals increased, and he moved out of Madinah to establish a farm. Initially, he would attend *Masjid Nabwi* for the prayers. As time passed, he got so busy with his business that he started missing the prayers in *Masjid Nabwi* and eventually stopped attending altogether. One day the Prophet ﷺ sent his companion to collect *zakat* from him (according to some scholars, it was Umar raḍiyallāhu 'anhu). The man said, "*Are you imposing a tax on me? Why should I give zakat*?" He then refused to pay it. The love of worldly treasures eventually took precedence over his priorities, and the man thus lost the rank of a companion.[10] His *zakat* was not accepted by the Prophet ﷺ or by the four caliphates afterwards.

---

10. Losing the rank of a companion of the Prophet ﷺ was the

We can compare this man's story to our current situation in the worldly life. As Mawlana Thanvi used to say, "It is okay to spend money on your food and have a home. It is also permissible to have comforts at your home. You can even decorate your home with the intention to please yourself (but not with the intention to flaunt your possessions). However, beyond this point leads to ostentation, and this is where one may fall into the ditch easily."

وَاعْلَمُوْٓا اَنَّمَآ اَمْوَالُكُمْ وَاَوْلَادُكُمْ فِتْنَةٌ ۙ وَّاَنَّ اللّٰهَ عِنْدَهٗٓ اَجْرٌ عَظِيْمٌ ﴿٢٨﴾

***And know that your possessions and your, children are but a trial and that surely, with Allah is a mighty reward.* (*al-Anfal 8: 28*)**

Our Prophet ﷺ used to pray to Allah ﷻ to make this world the least important to him. He used to ask for Allah's help to protect him from the mundane thoughts

---

greatest loss for this man. He gave up the rewards of the *Ākhirah*, and the higher status of becoming Prophet's ﷺ companion for the temporary gains and luxuries of this world. The companions of the Prophet ﷺ, also known as the Ṣaḥāba were the ones who stood with the Prophet ﷺ in difficult times. They were known for their piety, sacrifices, and virtuous character. Allah ﷻ bore witness to the purity of their hearts and their sincerity in faith, and mentioned them in the Qur'an as: "*Allah ﷻ was pleased with the believers when they were pledging allegiance with you (by placing their hands in your hands) under the tree, and He knew what was in their hearts, so He sent down tranquility upon them, and rewarded them with a victory, near at hand,*" (*al-Fath 48: 18*)

of collecting wealth. *Alhamdulillah*, Allah ﷻ has blessed us with enough resources, but we are busy acquiring more money and buying more clothes and worldly goods. This is what *fitna* (temptation) is. Do we think about earning enough good deeds to acquire the many blessings in *Jannah*, such as a magnificent house or flowing rivers under the gardens promised by Allah ﷻ?

Mawlana Rumi, an Islamic scholar and a *Sufi* poet, compared the life of a human being with a boat and his wealth with water in one of his poems. A person cannot live without money, and in the same way, a boat cannot sail without water. The boat moves smoothly only when the water is around it (surrounding it from the sides). If excess water comes inside, it destroys the boat. Similarly, if the world is around you, there is no harm. Make sure the water of this materialistic world does not enter the boat of your heart. If it does, the focus will only revolve around accumulating more possessions. This will lead to an endless road of temporal desires. Our stable finances are a blessing to us, and we should always be grateful to Allah ﷻ for it. May Allah ﷻ direct our thoughts toward the eternal life in *Jannah, āmīn.*

The Real Wealth

The biggest blessing in this life is the *īmān* (faith) given to us by Allah ﷻ which is our real wealth. Many people have to sacrifice a lot to achieve strong *īmān*. During the time of the Prophet ﷺ, the Muslims faced cruelty and oppression from the disbelievers of Makkah. Later, the Muslims of Chechnya, Bosnia, and Central Asia also withstood oppression but remained steadfast on the path of Allah ﷻ.

Currently, Muslims in Palestine, Kashmir, Burma, and East Turkestan are facing tyranny with the strength of their *īmān*. When I visited Uzbekistan a few years ago, the locals informed me that during the Soviet war, praying *ṣalāh* was considered a crime.[11] Towns were destroyed, and families were brutally martyred if the Holy Qur'an was found in their houses. Yet, the Muslims of Central Asia protected their *īmān* with utmost bravery. They lost their loved ones, wealth, and properties but stayed relentlessly steadfast on their *dīn*. On the other hand, we are blessed by being born into a home in a society where we can practise our *dīn* without trepidation. And for this, we should always thank Allah ﷻ and be grateful to Him.

---

11. During the Soviet regime, Islam was banned, and Muslims were not allowed to practise any Islamic ritual. *Salāh* was also forbidden, and it is reported that Muslims were executed for praying *ṣalāh*, not just inside the mosques, but also for praying in their homes.

Mufti Muhammad Hasan, a renowned scholar, used to say, "*Īmān* is the biggest wealth. Keep protecting it until you reach your grave, and you will be victorious in your *Ākhirah, Insha'Allah* ﷻ." It is because *īmān* is the deciding factor between our outcome in *Jannah* or *Jahannam.* Having *īmān* means a person has protection from the never-ending wrath of the Hellfire. This is important because polytheists will not be able to escape from *Jahannam.* For someone with *īmān*, no matter how sinful a person is, even though he may be punished initially for his sins, he eventually will be granted *Jannah* if he believed in the oneness of Allah ﷻ. Our Prophet ﷺ used to explain this concept using a beautiful example:[12]

Narrated by Abu Huraira: I heard Allah's Messenger ﷺ saying, "My example and the example of the people is that of a man who made a fire, and when it lighted what was around it, moths and other insects started falling into the fire. The man tried (his best) to prevent them (from falling into fire), but they overpowered him and rushed into the fire." The Prophet (ﷺ) added: "Now, similarly, I take hold of the knots at your waist (belts) to prevent you from falling into the Fire, but you insist on falling into it." (Ṣaḥīḥ al-Bukhari 6483)

There are two pathways in front of us, one is the path of *Shaytaan,* and the other is the path of Rahman. The path of *Shaytaan* has worldly desires, including fame, wealth, and so on. The one that goes to the Rahman

12. The salvation lies in following the commands of Allah ﷻ, through the Sunnah of the Prophet ﷺ who was given the responsibility to teach us the *dīn* of Allah ﷻ.

has trials and difficulties on it. It is the road of *sabr* that requires one to stay away from the forbidden acts, such as quarreling, telling lies, and overspending.

As humans, it is natural to get tempted to commit sins. Mawlana Thanvi explained this concept and connected it with our practise of fasting during Ramadan. He said, "If you are fasting and someone brings you a jug full of a cold beverage, you may feel like drinking it out of thirst, but you would never drink it because you know that you are fasting. You may have had a thought, but you did not act upon it." Therefore, when you are tempted to sin, first ask Allah ﷻ to protect you,[13] and remind yourself of the countless blessings Allah ﷻ has given you, such as your eyes, limbs, ears, tongue, *rizq*, home, family, and good health. Then encourage yourself to move away from the path of transgression with the complete trust that Allah ﷻ will save you from sin. This is the concept of *Mujaahida* (self-accountability), which brings us closer to Allah ﷻ. Getting closer to Allah ﷻ means possessing everything in this world and the Hereafter.[14]

---

13. In his other speeches, the shaykh, when explaining the concept of *taqwa* (the consciousness of Allah's presence), often narrates the story of Prophet Yusuf 'alayhi al-salām and how he asked Allah's help for protection against sins and said, "Maa'dh Allah," meaning 'I seek refuge with Allah ﷻ.' That is how we should also seek refuge with Allah ﷻ when tempted to sin.

14. The concept of *Tazkiyah, or Mujaahida* is a detailed topic on its own. In summary, it can be defined as the process of self-accountability where, a Muslim redefines the goal of their life and considers the ways and means to achieve the pleasure of Allah ﷻ, the manifestation of which will be granted in *Jannah*. It is the process of purification of the heart, and of one's lifestyle so one's heart and actions are aligned as per the commands of Allah ﷻ.

Tahajjud

Qiyam al-layl (the prayer of the night) is a great blessing.[15] It is neither *farḍ nor wājib*. Allah ﷻ has not mandated us to wake up at night and pray (if it was, I wonder how many of us would have been able to wake up and pray). *Tahajjud* is a Sunnah that strengthens our spirituality more than many other deeds. The blessings we get from praying *Tahajjud* are unimaginable.[16]

يَاَيُّهَا الْمُزَّمِّلُ ﴿١﴾ قُمِ الَّيْلَ اِلَّا قَلِيْلًا ﴿٢﴾ نِّصْفَهٗٓ اَوِ انْقُصْ مِنْهُ
قَلِيْلًا ﴿٣﴾ اَوْ زِدْ عَلَيْهِ وَرَتِّلِ الْقُرْاٰنَ تَرْتِيْلًا ﴿٤﴾

O you, wrapped up in clothes, stand at night (for prayer) except a little half of it, or make it a little less, or make it a little more; and recite the Qur'ān clearly with tartīl (in a distinct and measured tone).
(*al-Muzammil 73: 1-4*)

During the day, we are busy with everyday chores, and our minds are occupied with hundreds of thoughts. But in the depth of the night, during the last third, when we take time out to strengthen our connection with

15. Here, respected shaykh is talking about the *qiyam ul-layl* as well as *tahajjud*, however, the *bayan* is specifically on *tahajjud* prayer.
16. An important distinguishing factor between the prayer of *tahajjud* versus *qiyam ul-layl* is that *tahajjud* requires some sleep at night, as it means 'to rise from sleep' while *qiyam ul-layl* means to pray at night without having slept at any time of the night.

Allah ﷻ, we are endowed with special blessings and rewards.

Abu Huraira reported that the Prophet ﷺ said, "Our Lord Almighty descends to the lowest heaven in the last third of every night, saying: "Who is calling upon Me that I may answer him? Who is asking from Me that I may give him? Who is seeking My forgiveness that I may forgive him?" (Ṣaḥīḥ al-Bukhari 1145)

When one-third of the night is over, Allah ﷻ descends to the lowest Heaven. An opportunity is given to us to ask for *maghfirah* (forgiveness) and *aafiyah* (wellness). This announcement continues until the time of *Fajr*. Those who wake up to have a conversation with their Creator, in the form of *du'ā'*, are blessed with abundant favours. It is a precious time kept by Allah ﷻ.[17] The Prophet ﷺ used to encourage his companions to pray *Tahajjud*.

Abdullah ibn Umar رضي الله عنه narrates his story:

In the lifetime of the Prophet ﷺ, whosoever saw a dream would narrate it to Allah's Messenger ﷺ. I wished to see a dream that I could share with him. Once I saw in

---

17. The *Qur'an* has mentioned the characteristics of the servants of *Rahmaan*, one of which is that they get up at night and perform the *salah* of *Tahajjud*. (al-Furqān 25: 64) *Tahajjud* is a source of great spiritual energy. The Prophet ﷺ said, "You must perform the night prayer for it is the habit of the righteous who came before you; it brings you closer to your Lord, it expiates your evil deeds, and prevents you from sinning." (Tirmidhi 3549)

a dream that two angels caught hold of me and took me to the Fire which was built like a well and had two poles in it, and the people in it were known to me. I started saying, "I seek refuge with Allah ﷻ from the Fire." Then I met another angel who told me not to be afraid. I narrated the dream to Hafsa, (his sister, and the wife of Prophet ﷺ) who told this to Allah's Messenger ﷺ. The Prophet ﷺ said, "Abdullah is a good man. I wish he prayed *Tahajjud.*" After that Abdullah ibn Umar raḍiyallāhu 'anhu used to sleep but a little at night. (Ṣaḥīḥ al-Bukhari 1121, 1122)

This is how much our Prophet ﷺ wished for his ummah to pray *Tahajjud.* It is loved by Allah ﷻ, and we must make it a habit of waking up for it.

One may ask how flawed and feeble individuals like us can obtain the benefits of *Tahajjud*? Scholars often divide the night into three parts. The third half of the night is good for *Tahajjud.* One can perform the *ṣalāh*, go to bed, and wake up again for *Fajr*. Another way is to wake up in the third half of the night and not sleep afterwards. If neither can be done, one can make a habit of praying some extra *rakah* after *Isha* wsith the intention of waking up at night. There is no fixed number of *rakah* for *Tahajjud.* We can pray as many *rakah* as we can (two, four, six, or more).

Waking up in the middle of the night may be difficult and daunting, however, it is feasible. A renowned scholar once suggested useful points to his students about waking up for *Tahajjud.* He said, "Oftentimes, we wake up at night, either from a minor interruption in our sleep or to use the bathroom. This is the time to sit on the bed for a few minutes. As you sit, remind yourself that it is the hour when almighty Allah ﷻ is granting forgiveness. As you think about it, start praying for forgiveness and pray to Allah ﷻ to wake you up for *Tahajjud* and then go back to sleep. If done with true intention, Allah ﷻ will give you the strength to pray *Tahajjud Insha'Allah* ﷻ.

One of my teachers had a habit of performing a two-hour-long *dhikr* every night. Once, his body was unusually tired when he woke up for *Tahajjud*. He was eighty years old at that time, and his *nafs* told him that *Tahajjud* is not mandatory, and that sleep is crucial. So why not go back to bed or else he may get weak? Now the conversation started between him and his *nafs*. My teacher said, "Yes, it is true that sleep is important and sometimes we need more rest than usual, but this is the time when the Lord blesses the ones who wake up and ask Him for forgiveness. So, it does not seem appropriate to stay in bed." He got up and started making *du'ā'*. He then tried to convince his *nafs* to get up and said, "We are making *du'ā'* but without *wuḍū'*, so how about if I make *wuḍū'* and then make *du'ā'*?" He got out of bed and performed *wuḍū'* and again spoke with his *nafs*, "Isn't it better that we make this *du'ā'* while sitting on the prayer mat than on the bed?" Then he walked towards his prayer mat, and as soon as he reached it, he said, '*Allāhu Akbar*' and started his *Tahajjud* prayer. This way, the scholar gently brought his *nafs* towards discipline.

Once we get regular in praying *Tahajjud*, we can choose a lengthy *Surah* to have a longer *qiyaam*. It is also recommended that after praying *Tahajjud*, we must use the special hour to do the *dhikr* of Allah ﷻ and send abundant *salawat* on the Prophet ﷺ. Ask Allah ﷻ for anything you want. However, do not limit your *du'ā'* to worldly desires, but also ask for *maghfirah* (forgiveness), and protection from the punishment of the grave and the Hellfire. Make supplication for your parents, your family, the sick, the oppressed, and for those who have departed from this world. It is the time when everyone else is asleep, and you have the honour of sitting in front of the King of the heavens and earth, Allah ﷻ.

Heedlessness

The simple meaning of *tawfiq* is to be enlightened with an ability to achieve success. It means that one is blessed with the quality of being dedicated on the right path. *Alhamdulillah*, Allah ﷻ has favoured us with the *tawfiq* to pray five times a day. This is indeed a huge blessing, and we all should be grateful for it. However, it is unfortunate that our prayers are not performed with the same focus and concentration as per the standards. We find it difficult to pray with the thought of seeing Allah ﷻ in front of us or thinking that Allah ﷻ is watching us like it is mentioned in one Hadith:

"Worship Allah ﷻ as if you see Him, and even though you do not see Him, He is watching you." (Ṣaḥīḥ al-Bukhari 4777).

When we begin our *ṣalāh*, it often feels as though a machine-like movement has started. We simply recite what we have memorized, while our mind is busy with random thoughts. Often, this brings us sadness and despair. The result of this is even worse because the efforts to improve the prayer are lost in anguish and hopelessness. Sometimes we cannot recall what we recited in the first or second *rakah*. Some people get so distant that they classify their prayers as nothing but mere physical movements of the body.

My teacher, Mawlana Arifi (may Allah ﷻ grant him *Jannah*), once enlightened me with valuable advice.

He said, "It is a fact that our prayers are not performed with the focus and dedication that is required, but is it not a blessing in itself that at least we are given the *tawfiq* of standing in front of Allah ﷻ? Many are not even blessed with that. Whatever *tawfiq* we have is not by us, but it is from Allah ﷻ who showers His mercy upon us. Therefore, instead of labelling our prayers as a physical activity and depreciating our efforts, we must be grateful for the *tawfiq* given to us by Allah ﷻ. We can do this by first acknowledging that we have not prayed to the standards set by Allah ﷻ. We must then sincerely repent for not being as focused as we should have been.[18]

Ghaflah, or inattentiveness, goes away when we develop the habit of saying *shukr* (for the *tawfiq*) and *istighfar* (on the neglect) after each prayer. During the prayer, our focus should be on the words of the *Qur'an*. For example, recall the meaning of *Alhumdulillahi Rabbil Aalimeen* and remember the answer of Allah ﷻ on every ayah of Surah al-Fatihah.[19] This is the most basic level

18. This is to bring humility in a believer's conduct: we are grateful that Allah ﷻ allowed us to come to the prayer, and at the same time we repent for not praying with the utmost focus and attention like we should have. Shaykh Usmani regarded this method of *shukr* and *istighfar* to be a cornerstone in disciplining *one's nafs*.

19. Here, Shaykh is recalling the Hadith about the recitation of Surah al-Fatihah and Allah's reply to each *ayah* that is recited. Abu Hurayrah narrated that the Prophet ﷺ said, "Allah ﷻ says, I have divided prayer between Myself and My servant into two halves, and My servant shall have what he has asked for. When the servant says, "All praise is due to Allah ﷻ, the Lord of the worlds." Allah ﷻ says, "My servant has praised Me." When he says, "The Gracious, the Merciful,"

of submission, and its purpose is to bring our focus back towards the recitation of the *Qur'an* whenever the mind wanders. That is why the Prophet ﷺ used to say *astaghfir-ullāh*, three times, after finishing the prayer. As humans, we tend to not fulfil all the rights of prayer. Therefore, when a person acknowledges that he has made some mistakes during the prayer and says *istighfar* for it, Allah ﷻ forgives His servant, and the prayer gets accepted. Saying *istighfar* wipes away the guilt and gives the courage to perform the next prayer correctly.

Shukr and *istighfar* are the keys to beautifying our prayers as Allah ﷻ has promised us in *Surah Ibrahim*, "I will certainly give you more if you are grateful." (*Ibrahim* 14: 7)

إِنَّ اللَّهَ لَا يُخْلِفُ الْمِيعَادَ ﴿٩﴾

***Verily, Allah does not back out of His promise* (*al-Imran 3: 9*)**

Allah ﷻ says, "My servant has exalted Me." When the servant says, "The Master of the Day of Judgement," Allah ﷻ replies, "My servant has glorified Me, and my servant has submitted to Me." When he says, "You alone do we worship, You alone do we seek help," When Allah ﷻ says, "This is between Me and My servant, and My servant will have what he has asked for." When he says, "Guide us to the straight path, the path of those You have bestowed Your Grace, not of those who have incurred Your wrath, nor of those who have gone astray," When Allah ﷻ says, "This is for My servant, and My servant will have what he has asked for." (Ṣaḥīḥ al-Muslim 395)

Once, the Prophet ﷺ was travelling with his companions. When the time for prayer came, our Prophet ﷺ asked Bilal to pronounce the *adhan* (call to prayer), and said, "O Bilal, give us rest with it." (Sunan Abi Dawud)

Our prayers enhance tranquility and calmness in the heart through constant *shukr* and *istighfar*. After finishing the prayer, we must sit for some time to do *dhikr*. Afterwards, we must perform a quick self-assessment on the quality of the prayer. For example, "How did I recite the *Surah*? Did I perform the *ruku'* and *sujood* properly? Did I focus on the meaning of what I was reciting? Was my mind preoccupied with worldly thoughts? Was I mindful that I was standing in front of Allah ﷻ and that He was watching me?"

قُلْ يٰعِبَادِيَ الَّذِيْنَ اَسْرَفُوْا عَلٰٓي اَنْفُسِهِمْ لَا تَقْنَطُوْا مِنْ رَّحْمَةِ
اللّٰهِ ۭ اِنَّ اللّٰهَ يَغْفِرُ الذُّنُوْبَ جَمِيْعًا ۭ اِنَّهٗ هُوَ الْغَفُوْرُ الرَّحِيْمُ ﴿٥٣﴾

***"Say: "O My servants who have transgressed against themselves, do not despair of the mercy of Allah. Indeed, Allah forgives all sins. Indeed, it is He who is the Forgiving, the Merciful."* (al-Zumar 39: 53)**

As long as we do the self-assessment after each prayer, we are protected from self-approbation. The self-assessment of our prayers also protects us from the complacent thoughts that we have fulfilled the rights of *'ibādah*. With this constant practise of self-reflection, *shukr*, and *istighfar*, and Allah's mercy, we may get blessed with *khushu'* (humility) and *khudu'* (veneration) in our prayers.

May Allah ﷻ help us practise *shukr* and *istighfar* in our daily lives, *āmīn*.

The Advice of Prophet Nuh ﷺ

Prophet Nuh ﷺ lived a long life of nine hundred and fifty years. He spent his entire time spreading the call of *tawḥīd*. When it was his time to depart from this world, he advised his son on the four objectives he should strive for. His advice was reminiscent of his life's teachings. The interpretation of his advice is as follows:

First, Nuh ﷺ instructed his son to recite the declaration of faith, *La ilaha illa Allah* – there is no god but Allah ﷻ.

La ilaha illa Allah means having a firm belief in the oneness of Allah ﷻ. Prophet Nuh ﷺ asked his son to do the *dhikr* of *La ilaha illa Allah* at all times because it is the most superior form of *dhikr*. If the sun, moon, and the universe were placed on one side of a weighing scale and *La ilaha illa Allah* on the other, then the side with *La ilaha illa Allah* would outweigh the former. *La ilaha illa Allah* is the greatest truth because it declares the belief that Allah ﷻ is the sole creator of everything.[20] It is the dividing line between *kufr* and *īmān* and was the call of all the previous Prophets (peace be upon them all). It is so important that all Muslims are encouraged to say *La ilaha illa Allah* on our deathbeds.

---

20. Narrated by Bukhari, on the authority of Abu Hurayrah, who reported that the Prophet ﷺ said, "Faith consists of more than sixty branches, the best of which is to declare that there is no god but Allah ﷻ, the least of which is to remove something harmful from the road, and modesty is a branch of faith." (Ṣaḥīḥ al-Bukhari 9)

It is narrated by Abu Dharr that the Messenger of Allah ﷺ said: "Jibril came to me and gave me glad tidings, that whoever dies without associating anything with Allah ﷻ, then he will enter Paradise. I said, "Even if he commits adultery and theft?" He said, "Yes." (Jami al-Tirmidhi 2644)

It means that the individual would first pay heavily for his sins (unless he is forgiven by Allah ﷻ), but eventually, he will be granted entrance to *Jannah*. May Allah ﷻ forgive us and grant us a straight path to *Jannah*.

The Prophet ﷺ said, "After some time, when the people of *Jannah* will be in *Jannah*, and the ones in Hellfire will be in *Jahannam*, Allah ﷻ will ask the angels to take out the people from *Jahannam* who said *La ilaha illa Allah* (even if their *īmān* was as little as a mustard seed). That is the power of *La ilaha illa Allah.*" (Jami' al-Tirmidhi 2593)

In the Western countries, there are people with different religions, but how many of them believe in the oneness of Allah ﷻ? There are those who deviated from the true path and made false additions to the teachings of Prophet Isa 'alayhi al-salām, and addressed him as the Son of God (*astaghfirullāh*). We also know the deviants who call Uzair 'alayhi al-salām the Son of God (*astaghfirullāh*). There are idol worshippers, and then there are people who do not believe in any God (athiests). How many people are there who believe in the *aqeedah* (belief) of *tawḥīd* and that Prophet Muhammad ﷺ is the last Prophet of Allah ﷻ? That is why our *īmān* carries supreme value.

It is our most valuable possession in this life. My teacher Mufti Muhammad Hasan (may Allah ﷻ grant him *Jannah*) once said, "*Īmān* is a huge blessing. Keep safeguarding it from *shirk* and evil until you reach your grave, and the rest will be easy afterwards."[21]

Recite *La ilaha illa Allah* as your daily *dhikr* when you walk, or do your daily chores, and even while resting. Make a habit of involving the *dhikr* of *La ilaha illa Allah* as much as possible. May Allah ﷻ make us amongst the ones who recite it with abundance.

The second instruction by Prophet Nuh ﷺ to his son is the *dhikr* of *Subhan'Allahi Wabihamdihi* – All glory is to Allah ﷻ and all praise is to Him.

Scholars have regarded the *dhikr* of *Subhan'Allahi Wabihamdihi* as the *dhikr* of everything on our planet. It is regarded as the *dhikr* of the trees, animals, insects, and even the things we consider non-living such as the sky, rocks, and mountains. Thus, all are busy praising Allah ﷻ.

Subhan'Allah signifies that Allah ﷻ is free from all the defects, and *wabihamdihi* means all glory and praise is for Allah ﷻ only. Whatever we admire, whether a

---

21. Shaykh Taqi Usmani often recalls this quote from his teacher, Mufti Muhammad Hasan, which explains its repetition in several of his bayan.

mountain, a tree, or someone's beauty, we are praising its creator, Allah ﷻ.[22]

تُسَبِّحُ لَهُ السَّمٰوٰتُ السَّبْعُ وَالْاَرْضُ وَمَنْ فِيْهِنَّ ۚ وَاِنْ مِّنْ شَيْءٍ اِلَّا يُسَبِّحُ بِحَمْدِهٖ وَلٰكِنْ لَّا تَفْقَهُوْنَ تَسْبِيْحَهُمْ ۚ اِنَّهٗ كَانَ حَلِيْمًا غَفُوْرًا ﴿٤٤﴾

***"The seven heavens and the earth and all that is therein, glorify Him and there is not a thing but glorifies His praise. But you understand not their glorification. Truly, He is Ever Forbearing, Oft-Forgiving."* (al-Isra 17: 44)**

Prophet Nuh ﷺ then enlightened his son regarding the two forbidden acts he should avoid: *shirk* (polytheism) and *kibr* (pride).

وَعِنْدَهٗ مَفَاتِحُ الْغَيْبِ لَا يَعْلَمُهَآ اِلَّا هُوَ ۚ وَيَعْلَمُ مَا فِي الْبَرِّ وَالْبَحْرِ ۚ وَمَا تَسْقُطُ مِنْ وَّرَقَةٍ اِلَّا يَعْلَمُهَا وَلَا حَبَّةٍ فِيْ ظُلُمٰتِ الْاَرْضِ وَلَا رَطْبٍ وَّلَا يَابِسٍ اِلَّا فِيْ كِتٰبٍ مُّبِيْنٍ ﴿٥٩﴾

---

22. Narrated by Bukhari, on the authority of Abu Hurayrah, who reported that the Prophet ﷺ said, "Whoever says *Subhan'Allahi Wabihamdihi* one hundred times a day will be forgiven for all his sins, even if they were as much as the foam of the sea." (Ṣaḥīḥ al-Bukhari 6405) It must be noted that according to the scholars, the sins mentioned in this *hadith* include all minor sins, for major sins are forgiven only through *tawbah* and *istighfar*.

***With Him are the keys of the Unseen. No one knows them but He. He knows what is in the land and the sea. No leaf ever falls but that He knows about it, and there is no grain in the dark layers of the earth or anything fresh or dry that is not recorded in a manifest book.* (*al-An'am 6: 59*)**

Alhumdulillah, as Muslims, we have a firm belief in the oneness of Allah ﷻ. However, the scholars have further elaborated on the concept of *tawḥīd.* It is said that *tawḥīd* not only means a firm belief in the oneness of Allah ﷻ, but also necessitates not owning any attachment or love for anything or anyone in our heart, more than our love for Allah ﷻ. Our expectations should only be from Allah ﷻ, and our fear too should only be of Allah ﷻ and not of anyone else. Having a firm belief that nothing in this world can harm us if it is not the decree of Allah ﷻ also comes under the concept of *tawḥīd.*

Once, the Prophet ﷺ was resting under a tree, and his companions were sitting at a distance. A polytheist came and picked up the Prophet's ﷺ sword. He placed it on the Prophet's neck and asked, "Who will save you now from me?" The Prophet ﷺ fearlessly said, "Allah ﷻ," and he ﷺ said it with such composure that the disbeliever dropped his sword. The Prophet ﷺ then picked it up and asked the man, "Who will save you now?" The man was so impressed by the firm belief and *tawakkul* (trust in Allah ﷻ) of our Prophet ﷺ that he embraced Islam (*SubhanAllah*). Such was the level of *tawḥīd,* and such was the *tawakkul* of our beloved Prophet ﷺ.

The final point mentioned by Prophet Nuh ﷺ concerns *kibr*, which means pride or arrogance. Our Prophet ﷺ regarded *kibr* as one of the biggest diseases in our society. It is so dangerous that the one who suffers from it is unaware of being affected by it. This is why we never find someone who is proud and also admits that he has the disease of *kibr*. Unfortunately, this disease paves a direct road to Hellfire.[23]

It is narrated by Abu Hurayrah that the Prophet ﷺ said, "Allah ﷻ says, "Pride is my cloak and greatness My robe, and he who competes with Me in respect of either of them, I shall cast into Hellfire." (40 Hadith Qudsi: 19)

Pride is like a cancer for our *īmān*. Unfortunately, in the modern world, the roots of ego and arrogance are growing deeper. Pride is the reason why *Iblīs* turned into a *Shaytaan*. *Iblīs* was once one of the most religious *jinns*, but when asked to prostrate to Adam ﷺ, he refused and said, "Why would I prostrate to a human who is made from clay? I am made from fire, and fire is better than clay." It was pride that made him *Shaytaan* and will eventually lead him to the Hellfire for eternity. Why is the disease of *kibr* so deadly? It is because once pride enters our hearts, it is very difficult to treat. Self-admiration and ego prevent an arrogant person from listening to any advice.

---

23. Scholars regard arrogance, jealousy, hatred, and the love of wealth as the four major sins of the soul. They divert a person from the path of *hidayah* (true guidance).

Kibr advances in three stages. The first stage is called *ujub*, self-conceitedness. It means thinking oneself as good, knowledgeable, and well-trained. The seed of pride begins silently, and the person first notices his good qualities. The second stage is *kibr*, where an individual thinks, "I am better than others." Now the person falls into the trap of superiority over others, such as in his education, ethnicity, financial status, or physical appearance. Until this stage, the emotions were inside, but the final stage accentuates this into actions. This stage is called *takabbur*, which means "practising pride". A few common examples include refusing to talk to people, showing pride in conversations (bragging about accomplishments), insulting, and throwing anger at others out of context, etc.

Abdullah narrated that the Prophet ﷺ said: "Whoever has pride (arrogance) in his heart, even as much as the size of a mustard seed's weight, shall not be admitted into Paradise." (Jami` at-Tirmidhi 1998)

So, how do we protect our hearts from *kibr*? The answer is straightforward. Whenever you think of any of your achievements, possessions, or good qualities (such as higher education, an esteemed position in your office or society, or your physical beauty), remind yourself that everything you have is a blessing from Allah ﷻ, and The One who gave it to you can take it away at any time.

We must remember how we arrived in this world. We came with no knowledge or possessions. It is Allah ﷻ Who blessed us with knowledge and wealth, and it is He who can take away these favours at any time. The same goes for beauty, health, and the strength that comes from Allah ﷻ. Saying *Alhamdulillah* for every blessing severs the roots of pride.

Suppose you borrow a beautiful dress from someone for a special occasion.[24] You like wearing it, and it looks good on you. Even though the dress makes you look good, you know that it does not belong to you, and the person can take it back at any moment. Will you be feeling any pride wearing that dress? Likewise, if you visit a luxurious palace, will you think that the palace belongs to you? No, because you are only a visitor there. The palace belongs to the king who can throw you out at any time. Such are the attributes we enjoy in this temporary world. We can never say we earned them because they are blessings from Allah ﷻ, and He can take them back when He wills. The key is to keep reminding ourselves of this truth and say *Alhamdulillah* whenever we think of our good qualities.

Jabir bin Abdullah said that he heard the Prophet ﷺ say, "The best of remembrance is *La ilaha illa Allah* (None has the right to be worshipped but Allah ﷻ), and the best of supplication is *Alhamdulillah* (praise is to Allah ﷻ)." (Sunan ibn Majah 3800)

---

24. Shaykh Usmani's lectures are remarkable because he uses everyday examples to illustrate his points. Here, he draws our attention to the clothes we wear and how they are connected to the blessings of Allah ﷻ. He emphasizes that everything we own and all that we spend comes from Allah ﷻ, and that Allah ﷻ has the power to take it away from us at any moment.

The Consciousness of Allah's Presence

Taqwa is one of the most virtuous characteristics a true believer can have.[25] It has been reiterated multiple times in the Qur'an,

وَاعْلَمُوٓا اَنَّ اللّٰهَ يَعْلَمُ مَا فِيٓ اَنْفُسِكُمْ فَاحْذَرُوْهُ ۚ وَاعْلَمُوٓا اَنَّ اللّٰهَ غَفُوْرٌ حَلِيْمٌ ﴿٢٣٥﴾

***And know that Allah knows what is within yourselves, so beware of Him. And know that Allah is Forgiving and Forbearing.* (*al-Baqarah 2: 235*)**

Practising *taqwa* gets easier when we implement this notion in our everyday life. As an outcome, we are endowed with endless blessings from unimaginable sources. *Taqwa* makes us obey Allah's orders in all areas of our life. At present, our societies have well-defined legislation and well-equipped law enforcement agencies. There are enactments for nearly every criminal activity, including burglary, alcohol abuse, drug abuse, murder, fornication, corruption, and bribery. Despite this, criminal offenses and immorality are very prevalent around us. There is lawlessness and degeneracy everywhere.

25. Often regarded as the fear of Allah ﷻ, *taqwa*, in its literal sense, means that one is conscious of Allah's presence around us. It means that the person is aware they of being watched and heard by Allah ﷻ at all times.

Why is that? It is because there is a decline in moral values and no fear of Allah's ﷻ accountability and wrath.

وَلَقَدْ خَلَقْنَا الْإِنْسَانَ وَنَعْلَمُ مَا تُوَسْوِسُ بِهِ نَفْسُهُ ۖ وَنَحْنُ أَقْرَبُ إِلَيْهِ مِنْ حَبْلِ الْوَرِيدِ ﴿١٦﴾

***And indeed, We have created man, and We know whatever thoughts his inner self develops, and We are closer to him than (his) jugular vein.* (*Qāf 50: 16*)**

The above verse in Surah Qaf reminds us of *taqwa.* Allah ﷻ has instructed us to practise it. But what exactly is *taqwa*? There are many meanings and understandings of this word. The Arabic meaning of *taqwa* is fear (of Allah ﷻ), forbearance, and abstinence. However, the in-depth meaning of *taqwa* is to have the consciousness that our time in this world is limited. *Taqwa* is to have a mindset that one day we all will be answerable to Our Lord for everything we did during our lifetime. The awareness of always being watched brings mindfulness of Allah's presence. As a result, every act is done vigilantly. The one with *taqwa* thinks about his action: is it going to please Allah ﷻ or is it going to make Him angry? Is the action going to be accepted as a good deed or not?

وَأَسِرُّوا قَوْلَكُمْ أَوِ اجْهَرُوا بِهِ ۖ إِنَّهُ عَلِيمٌ بِذَاتِ الصُّدُورِ ﴿١٣﴾

***And conceal your speech or publicize it; indeed, He is Knowing of that within the chests.* (*al-Mulk 67: 13*)**

Today there are closed-circuit cameras installed wherever we go. It is common to see a sign that says, "You are on camera" or "You are being watched".[26] A small camera is enough to make us conscious of our movements, even when we are not doing anything wrong. But what about our Creator who is watching us at all times? The security camera notices our physical attributes and monitors any suspicious activity, but it cannot monitor what we are thinking inside. However, when it comes to Allah ﷻ, He is not only aware of the physical aspect, but He also knows what's inside our hearts and our minds. *Subhan'Allah.* If *taqwa* is inside our hearts, we will always do what Allah ﷻ has enjoined and avoid what He has forbidden.

Life is spent in *ghaflah* (neglect or heedlessness) if the seed of *taqwa* is not planted in the heart, and it may display itself in an individual who travels to different places or indulges in activities without contemplating whether he is practising *halal* or *haram*. Such is a state of *ghaflah*, where a person is living his life without any self-assessment. It is like being in a pitch-dark cavern.[27] *Taqwa*, on the other hand, is the opposite of *ghaflah* and should be applied to all aspects of our life, for example, when we

---

26. When explaining this point, Shaykh Usmani recalled his time at the NASA museum in Houston, Texas. He encountered a security sign that said, "You are being watched," and the Shaykh recalled the watchfulness of his deeds by the two angels and also by Allah ﷻ. Such is the *taqwa* of our scholars, who recall Allah ﷻ at all times, even while exploring a museum.

27. In the darkness of a cave, it's difficult to see one's hands or feet, and so one cannot appreciate his bodily movements.

are performing ablution or *wuḍu'*. *Taqwa* is to observe whether one is doing *wuḍu'* the correct way that is according to the *Sunnah*. Is the amount of water appropriate, or am I wasting it? Am I starting it with *Bismillah*? Is the tap turned on for too long? *Taqwa* is to remember what our Prophet ﷺ said about *wuḍu'*.

The Prophet ﷺ once passed by his companion Sa'd, who was performing ablution. The Prophet ﷺ said, "What is this extravagance?" Sa'd said, "Is there extravagance with water in ablution?" The Prophet ﷺ replied, "Yes, even if you were on the banks of a flowing river." (Musnad Ahmad 7065)[28]

There is no scarcity of water in the flowing river, but the Prophet ﷺ still advised us not to waste it to highlight the significance of water. Remembering this *Hadith* while performing *wuḍhū'* is *taqwa*, and it brings us closer to Allah ﷻ. Unfortunately, people in developing nations face a shortage of water, electricity and gas. To an extent, this problem can be solved if people follow the advice of the Prophet ﷺ and refrain from wasting resources.

Imam al-Shafi, a great scholar of *Hadith* and *fiqh* (Islamic jurisprudence), was blessed with a high level of *taqwa*.[29] Whenever he was asked a question on *fiqh*,

---

28. Shaykh Usmani often recalls *ahadith* on *israaf* owing to its commonality in our society. Readers may thus find some of these *ahadith* repeated in different *bayan*.

29. *Taqwa* must also be practised when spreading knowledge. Scholars of the past observed *taqwa* even when asked simple questions. One example is Imam al-Shafi, who has been quoted here by the Shaykh.

it was his habit to remain silent for a few minutes and then answer the query. Someone once asked him the reason for taking short intervals before answering and Imam al-Shafi said that he does so to take time to reflect on whether his answer would lead him to *Jannah* or *Jahannam*. Once he gets the clarity, he then answers the question. *Subhan'Allah*, may Allah ﷻ also bless us with such *taqwa*.

Now let's recall the carefree gatherings where no one is bothered whether their speech includes any *gheebah* or if they are mocking someone. This is where *taqwa* is needed. Doing good deeds and respecting Almighty Allah's commands should go hand in hand. Take the example of breathing. We breathe in two parts. First, we breathe in air that goes into the lungs, and then breathe it out and release it to complete one breath. Suppose you breathe in but cannot breathe out. Or you cannot take the next breath. It is an act of extreme ingratitude that even though we are constantly showered with blessings, yet we continue to indulge in what is prohibited.[30] May Allah ﷻ help us practise *taqwa* in our lives, *āmīn*.

---

30. The respected Shaykh is pointing towards the blessings of Allah ﷻ on our bodies, which we usually do not take into account, and often show ingratitude by using these blessings in wrong actions. For example, Allah ﷻ has blessed us with a tongue that performs multiple roles. It helps us with speech, provides taste through thousands of tastebuds, and works with the salivary glands in the mouth to keep it moist. A heedless servant of Allah ﷻ, in his neglect, may use the same tongue in lying, backbiting and foul speech, thus portraying extreme ingratitude to the blessing.

يَاَيُّهَا الَّذِيْنَ اٰمَنُوا اتَّقُوا اللّٰہَ وَابْتَغُوْٓا اِلَيْہِ الْوَسِيْلَۃَ وَجَاہِدُوْا فِيْ
سَبِيْلِہٖ لَعَلَّكُمْ تُفْلِحُوْنَ ۝۳۵

***O you who believe! Do your duty to Allah and fear Him. And seek the waseela (means of approach to Him) and strive hard in His Cause (as much as you can), so that you may be successful.* (*al-Mai'dah 5: 35*)**

Windows of Sin

All praise and glory is to Allah ﷻ Who blessed us with the jewel of *imān*.[31] *Alhamdulillah*, most of us are born into a Muslim family, and we face no impediments in practising our *dīn*. Frequently, we see that in some households, religion is practised only upon the demise of a family member. *Alhamdulillah*, we are born in a family where the remembrance of Allah ﷻ is present.[32] Because of this, we often think that our way to *Jannah* is easy, that the prayers and fasts will promptly escort us to the eternal gardens, and that there is no need to do anything supplementary. This complacent attitude is called *ghaflah* (heedlessness). There must never be a time for a Muslim to feel self-satisfied in strengthening the bond with Allah ﷻ. The journey of *dhikr* and the road towards Allah ﷻ is endless, and the soul must trudge ceaselessly to succeed in this journey.

وَالَّذِيْنَ يُؤْتُوْنَ مَآ اٰتَوْا وَّقُلُوْبُهُمْ وَجِلَةٌ اَنَّهُمْ اِلٰى رَبِّهِمْ رٰجِعُوْنَ ﴿٦٠﴾

And those who give what they give while their hearts (are) fearful, because they to their Lord (will) return. **(*al-Mu'minoon 23: 60*)**

---

31. Shaykh Mufti Taqi Usmani often starts his *bayan* with the *shukr* for the blessings of Allah ﷻ. Here, he is saying the *shukr* for the blessing of *Īmān* and to be a part of the *ummah* of the beloved Prophet ﷺ.

32. It must be noted that this address was for the students and attendees at Darul Uloom, Karachi, where the audience is often from religiously practising backgrounds.

We think that backbiting and lying are the only two ways our tongues are involved in transgressions, but that is not the case. Our tongues are can encompass unrestrained sinning if we are unaware of its use. On the Day of Judgment, our eyes will testify to Allah ﷻ about the sins they committed because of our *nafs*. The tongue will mention all the *gheebah* and lying we perpetrated.[34]

حَتّٰىٓ اِذَا مَا جَاۤءُوْهَا شَهِدَ عَلَيْهِمْ سَمْعُهُمْ وَاَبْصَارُهُمْ وَجُلُوْدُهُمْ بِمَا
كَانُوْا يَعْمَلُوْنَ ﴿٢٠﴾ وَقَالُوْا لِجُلُوْدِهِمْ لِمَ شَهِدْتُّمْ عَلَيْنَا ۗ قَالُوْٓا اَنْطَقَنَا
اللّٰهُ الَّذِيْٓ اَنْطَقَ كُلَّ شَيْءٍ وَّهُوَ خَلَقَكُمْ اَوَّلَ مَرَّةٍ وَّاِلَيْهِ تُرْجَعُوْنَ ﴿٢١﴾

Until, when they reach it, their hearing and their eyes and their skins will testify against them of what they used to do. And they will say to their skins, "Why have you testified against us?" They will say, "We were made to speak by Allah, who has made everything speak; and He created you the first time, and to Him, you are returned. **(*al-Fussilat 41: 20-21*)**

A lot of the times, this is not even considered to be deplorable in our society. We witness or are involved in deceiving each other just for an escapade amongst people. We relish in this, lacking the basic understanding that the tongue and ears are going astray for petty worldly amusement. Another example customary to our

34. Five organs will testify on the day of Judgement. It includes the tongue, hands, feet (as mentioned in Surah *al-Nur* 24: 24 and Surah *Yasin* 36: 65), eyes, and ears (as mentioned in Surah *Fussilat* 41: 20).

society is spreading information without confirming the facts first. This has become a norm nowadays. My father used to comment, "When you talk about a matter, such as an announcement or a disclosure about an event, envision yourself defending it in a court of law. Will you be able to prove the truth regarding what you convey? This is because the final court of justice on the Day of *Qiyamah* will ask you to provide proof."

Today, we are oblivious to the certainty that we are always being recorded. The consciousness of every word spoken, whether it is good or bad, is registered, and is dwindling in our communities. How much of what we spoke was true and what was counterfeited will all be counted. Once let loose, our tongues becomes an unbridled horse that gets very laborious to rein. So, what's the solution in such circumstances? It is to speak less and to think before you speak. Speak to bring benefit to others; otherwise staying silent is the key to serenity. May Allah ﷻ help us in achieving eternal success, *āmīn*.

Our Friends, Shukr and Du‘ā’

Health and well-being are the treasures of this blessed life. The gateway that ushers an individual to the remembrance of Allah ﷻ unlatches in the course of illness and affliction. Disability compels one to understand the significance of prosperity. In our contemporary world, we acknowledge the scientific and architectural wonders around us. However, the most extraordinary marvel and masterpiece is the body of the human being. Every segment of our body accommodates a world of unfathomable intricate details one cannot imagine.

وَقُلِ الْحَمْدُ لِلّٰهِ سَيُرِيْكُمْ اٰيٰتِهٖ فَتَعْرِفُوْنَهَا ۭ وَمَا رَبُّكَ بِغَافِلٍ عَمَّا تَعْمَلُوْنَ ﴿٩٣﴾

***And say, "Praise belongs to Allah. He will show you His signs, then you will recognize them. And your Lord is not unaware of what you do."* (*al-Naml 27: 93*)**

لَقَدْ خَلَقْنَا الْاِنْسَانَ فِيْٓ اَحْسَنِ تَقْوِيْمٍ ﴿٤﴾

***We have certainly created man in the best of stature.* (*al-Tīn 95: 4*)**

Human beings are created in a more superior way compared to any other creation of Allah ﷻ. The human body, a paragon of wonder, is more beautiful than the sun, the moon and the stars. Observe your face and notice your features. We all have similar attributes on our faces, including two eyes, two ears, a mouth, and a nose, and yet every face is different from the other. From the time of Prophet Adam ﷺ until today, no two countenances are created exactly alike *Subhana'Allah.* Every feature, including our voice, facial characteristics, and fingerprints, is distinct from other individuals. Billions of humans have been born since the beginning of time. As we observe diverging ethnicities, we can distinguish the homogeneous traits of pigmentation of the skin, eyes, hair, etc. The Arabs look different from Caucasians, and Africans are different from Asians. There are analogies and divergence at the same time.

The human body is like a museum of remarkable organs. Inside every organ is a factory silently performing its allegiance. Take the example of our eyes. Allah ﷻ the almighty has delineated such complex details in them that we have more than five different sub-specialties in the field of ophthalmology. There is a physician specializing in the management of glaucoma, another for cataract, then retina, and so on. The same detail applies to other organs of our body. During an angiography procedure, the blood vessels supplying blood to the heart are visualized. They are thin as threads, and their obstruction can cause a massive heart attack. These narrow vessels function ceaselessly during our lifetime, sometimes for seventy years or more. Therefore, it is important to be perpetually grateful for the blessing of health.[35]

---

35. Shaykh Mufti Taqi Usmani is known for his *bayan's* simplicity and for bringing our attention to forgotten matters, such as being grateful for a healthy body.

The minimum we can do is to say *Alhamdulillah* for our eyes, nose, tongue, and rest of our functional body.[36] We find ourselves closer to Allah ﷻ when we say *shukr* for all the blessings and favours bestowed by Him.

My father once visited one of his relatives, who was suffering from a severe toothache. She was an elderly lady who was known for her piety and God-fearing qualities. She said to him, "Brother, our teeth give pain when they erupt in the prepubescent period as well as when falling out during senescence". He responded, "Sister, you only remember the agony and discomfort you get from your teeth. Do you not recall the amount of food you devoured with them for the last six or seven decades?" This is how we all are. We have eyes, ears, hands and legs. But how often are we grateful to Allah ﷻ for them?

We must value our time when we are healthy because *shukr* is not just from the heart and tongue but also from our deeds. *Shukr* from the executed acts is by utilizing our blessings in the cause of Allah ﷻ. Use your eyes for good, such as to look at your parents,[37] read and

---

36. *Anas ibn Malik* reported that the Prophet ﷺ said, "Allah ﷻ does not bestow His bounties upon a servant and the servant says, *Alhamdulillah* (All praise is due to Allah ﷻ), but that what he has given for praise is better than what he has taken of bounties." (Sunan Ibn Mājah 3805)

37. Kindness to one's parents by fulfilling their rights, serving them and making them happy is one of the most beloved deeds to Allah ﷻ. It is mentioned in *surah Luqman* that 'We commanded man (to be good) in respect of his parents.' (Luqman 31: 14). It is narrated by *Abdullah ibn Amr ibn A'as* that once a man came to the Prophet ﷺ and asked for permission to participate in *jihad*. The Prophet ﷺ asked him if any

study the Qur'an, and see the Holy *Ka'ba*. Use your tongue to praise the greatness of the Almighty, Who created this delightful world. Do not use it to offend anyone, do *gheebah*, or utter foul language. Do not use your ears to listen to music or *gheebah*.

The other special gift given to us is *du'ā'*. In our society, du'ā' has been limited to certain acts of worship, such as after *ṣalāh* or when visiting Masjid *al-Haraam*. But du'ā' is like an undeviating train that reaches its destination without any interruptions. It is one of the easiest routes that brings us closer to Allah ﷻ. Furthermore, we do not need any outstanding curriculum or training to make *du'ā'*. Once, a companion asked the Prophet ﷺ to guide him with a concise piece of advice that is easy to follow. The Prophet ﷺ stated that he must always do the *dhikr* of Allah ﷻ on his tongue. An effortless way of incorporating the *dhikr* is by constant *du'ā'* and *shukr*.

When we learn the *Qur'an*, we observe that the entire *Qur'an* can be summarized in one *Surah*, known to us as Surah al-Fatihah. It is the opening chapter of the Qur'an, indispensable for our *ṣalāh*. Without *Surah al-Fatihah*, our *ṣalāh* is invalid. Why is this *Surah* so essential? It is because Surah *al-Fatihah* is a beautiful combination of *shukr* and *du'ā'*.

---

of his parents were alive. The man said, "Yes, both of them are alive." The Prophet ﷺ said to the man, "Then exert yourself in their service." (Ṣaḥīḥ al-Bukhari 3004). Thus, Shaykh Usmani is pointing towards the rights of parents and the reward of looking after them and serving them in the best of ways.

إِيَّاكَ نَعْبُدُ وَإِيَّاكَ نَسْتَعِينُ ﴿٤﴾

You alone do we worship, and from You alone do we seek help. (al-Fatihah 1: 5)

We must make a habit of asking from Allah ﷻ at all times. *Du‘ā’* is a form of *ibādah* that reinforces our relationship with Allah ﷻ. Upon rising in the morning, pray to Allah ﷻ for a blessed day, which you will spend pleasing Him. When preparing to eat, make *du‘ā’* for an appetizing meal filled with *barakah*. Before going to the market, ask Allah ﷻ to save you from wasting money and time. In a gathering with friends, pray that Allah ﷻ protects you from *gheebah*. The only way to get protection from the evils of this world is to direct our hearts towards Allah ﷻ, through *du‘ā’* and *shukr*.

May Allah ﷻ guide us to involve these two actions consistently in our daily life, *āmīn*.

Remembrance of Allah

ٱلَّذِينَ ءَامَنُوا۟ وَتَطْمَئِنُّ قُلُوبُهُم بِذِكْرِ ٱللَّهِ ۗ أَلَا بِذِكْرِ ٱللَّهِ تَطْمَئِنُّ ٱلْقُلُوبُ ﴿٢٨﴾

***The ones who believe and their hearts are peaceful with the remembrance of Allah. Surely, the hearts find peace only in the remembrance of Allah.* (*al-Ra'd 13: 28*)**

In the above *ayah*, Allah ﷻ is designating the significance of His remembrance and is asking the believers to praise their Lord. This message is for those who believe in Allah ﷻ, Allah's Prophets, and the *Ākhirah*. The question arises, why is the command of Allah's *dhikr* given to us? Is it going to provide any benefit to the Creator? (*mādhAllah*)[38] or is the Almighty in need of any *dhikr*? (*mādhAllah*). The magnificence of Almighty Allah ﷻ is not affected by the presence or absence of humans, nor does He need our supplications and prayers. The remembrance of Allah ﷻ is in fact imperative for the wellness of mankind. One of the major benefits is that *dhikr* increases our rank in the *Ākhirah*.

The remembrance of Allah ﷻ protects us from wrongful pursuits. Today, we can see injustice, transgressions, degeneracy and criminal activities commonly

38. Meaning "I seek refuge with Allah ﷻ."

practised in the Muslim world. One of its fundamental causes is the scarcity of the *dhikr* of Allah ﷻ in our society. When someone is involved in a crime, he is oblivious to the fact that Allah ﷻ is watching him. An individual takes usury for a better lifestyle but is unconcerned about the day when we all will be answerable to Allah ﷻ about our wealth. Being unmindful about the Almighty and accountability on the Day of *Qiyamah* leads to corruption and immorality. We often perceive that poverty generates a rise in the crime rates, but we also see corruption being more common among the riches. Unfortunately, we have forgotten the concept of *Jahannam.*

On the other hand, someone who remembers the *Ākhirah,* and the interrogations on the day of *Qiyamah* will be less likely to commit unlawful activities. There are examples in our society where some people reject prohibited luxuries and live modestly because of their consciousness of the *Ākhirah.*

The Prophet ﷺ once said, "If the son of Adam had a valley full of gold, he would want to have two valleys. Nothing fills his mouth but the dust of the grave, yet Allah ﷻ will relent to whoever repents to Him." (Ṣaḥīḥ Bukhari 6075)

In this *Hadith*, the Prophet ﷺ is delineating the human nature of acquiring wealth. Only the soil of the grave satisfies the heart that is greedy for more money, a higher rank and status. The valley of gold (in the *Hadith*) is equivalent to coveting a larger house or a business unit in our time. The only way to liberate oneself from worldly temptations and unnecessary extravagance is by remembering Allah ﷻ and the Day of *Qiyamah*. *Halal* earning brings contentment to the heart that flourishes with the *dhikr* of Allah ﷻ.

How do we bring the *dhikr* of Allah ﷻ into our lives? There are various techniques explained and practised by our Prophet ﷺ. One that was stressed specifically is the constant supplication in the daily routine. For example, starting the day with a *du'ā'*:

اَلْحَمْدُ لِلّٰهِ الَّذِىْ أَحْيَانَا بَعْدَ مَا أَمَاتَنَا وَ إِلَيْهِ النُّشُوْرُ

Praise is to Allah Who gives us life after He has caused us to die and to Him is the return.
(*Ṣaḥīḥ al-Bukhari 6324*)

Sleep is a minor form of death because the soul is taken when a person sleeps. Every morning, Allah ﷻ gives us another chance to rectify our matters. The second part of the *du'ā'* (وَ إِلَيْهِ النُّشُوْرُ) means that we all will be returning to Allah ﷻ. The first lesson this *du'a* gives us upon waking up, is about our guaranteed departure from this world, when we will return to Allah ﷻ. What we do in the day should revolve around the concept of *du'ā'* recited upon waking up.

Second, when entering the bathroom, recite:

اَللّٰهُمَّ إِنِّىْ أَعُوْذُبِكَ مِنَ الْخُبُثِ وَ الْخَبَائِثِ

***(In the name of Allah). O Allah, I take refuge with you from all evil and evil-doers.* (Ṣaḥīḥ Bukhari 142)**

When coming out of the bathroom, we say

غُفْرَ انَکَ

***I ask You (Allah) for forgiveness.* (Sunan Abi Dawud 30)**

In the same way, there are specific *du'ā'* for particular emotions, actions and activities. For example, there is a *du'ā'* before and after eating, during travel, when feeling angry or anxious, when entering and leaving the home, and so on. This is how our beloved Prophet ﷺ taught us the remembrance of Allah ﷻ in our daily routine. Unfortunately, we do not realize the value of it, but these supplications are a great way of maintaining a strong connection with Allah ﷻ as it always keeps Him in our minds. Nowadays, we have booklets on short supplications easily available to us. As Muslims, we must memorize them with their translation and include them in our daily routine.

وَقَالَ رَبُّكُمُ ادْعُوْنِيٓ اَسْتَجِبْ لَكُمْ

***And your Lord says, "Call upon Me; I will respond to you."* (al-Mu'min 40: 60)**

The importance of constant supplication is highlighted in another *Hadith*.

Anas ibn Malik reported: The Messenger of Allah ﷺ said, "Let one of you ask his Lord for his needs, all of them, even for a shoestring when his breaks." (Tirmidhī 3973)

The Prophet ﷺ is telling us to ask Allah ﷻ even if our shoelace needs fixing. We know that in order to mend the shoe, one must look for a shoe repair store or a cobbler. However, asking Allah ﷻ to help us find them would include the remembrance of Allah ﷻ in the task. Likewise, when going out or driving, make *du'ā'*, to reach the destination safely. Also, recite the supplication for leaving the house and the *du'ā'* for travelling made by our Prophet ﷺ. When entering a restaurant, make *du'ā'* that Allah ﷻ provides you with a satisfying meal. When going to your workplace, make *du'ā'* that you have a productive day. Thus, supplicating in every step is one of the most expeditious ways to strengthen our connection with Allah ﷻ. To make it into a habit needs some practise, but once we are involved in the remembrance of Allah ﷻ, everything in life will fall into place, Insha'Allah ﷻ.[39]

May Allah ﷻ guide us and make us live the way that is beloved to Him, *āmīn*.

---

39. Here, Shaykh is bringing our attention to the *ayah* of the *Qur'an* where Allah ﷻ says, "I did not create jinn and humans except to worship Me." (*Adh-Dhariyat* 51: 56) By involving in the *dhikr* of Allah ﷻ, even the mundane tasks of daily life can be turned into an *'ibādah*. Thus, a person remains connected with Allah ﷻ even when involved in daily chores.

The Five Questions

Once, the Prophet ﷺ was at home, and he ﷺ was feeling hungry, but there was nothing to eat. He decided to visit the garden of one of his *Ansār* companions. It was summertime, so the temperature was hot, which was the ideal time for the ripening of palm dates. The companion was pleased to see the Prophet ﷺ and served him some palm dates and water. Upon having the snack, the Prophet ﷺ said, “In the *Qur’an*, Allah ﷻ has mentioned that we will be asked about all the blessings bestowed on us by Him, and that also includes the palm dates I ate and the water I drank”.

In other words, we will be questioned about all the small and big favours given to us by Allah ﷻ. There are two salient points to remember here. Firstly, we must be grateful to Allah ﷻ for the blessings, and secondly, we must stay away from transgression and *haram*. The blessings we have been granted by Allah ﷻ have their own rights and entitlement. Take the example of our eyes. We did not pay for them, and the right of the blessing of vision is to be grateful for it and not to use them to commit sins such as watching *haram* content or not lowering our gaze. The life that we currently live, as per our *īmān*, is symbolized by a preparatory phase with multitudinous tests. The objective is to prepare the individuals for the final exam in front of Allah ﷻ. However, the questions for the exam have already been disclosed to us. We must follow the *Qur’an* and *Sunnah* so we are successful.

Our Prophet ﷺ once mentioned, "Ibn-e-Adam (children of Adam) will not be able to move their feet until they answer the five questions." (Jami' al-Tirmidhi 2416)

Here, the Prophet ﷺ is referring to not being able to move when we shall be standing on the Bridge of *Sirāt* with *Jahannam* under it and *Jannah* in front of it. Everyone would desire to enter *Jannah*, but they will not shift until they answer the five questions. The noble answers will bring *Jannah* as the destination, and God forbid if the responses are negative, *Jannah* gets farther away, and *Jahannam* comes closer.

Take the example of a student. If a student discovers what is coming in the finals, he will strive to do the best preparation and give the best answers. Allah ﷻ has given us the exam paper through the Prophet ﷺ. But it is important to remember that you will give the answers according to how you lived your life on Earth.[40] So, let's go over the questions we will be asked:

First question: How did we spend our life?

40. Sometimes, people argue that we should be given another chance to come back to life and rectify our matters. Scholars often explain it by providing examples of worldly exams. The idea of a second chance may seem reasonable if the exam questions were hidden or no guidance was provided. However, in the life of this world, Allah ﷻ not only provided us with a guidebook (the *Qur'an*) but also informed us of the exam questions through the Prophet ﷺ.

Allah ﷻ blesses human beings to exist. Usually, a human has a long life consisting of several decades.[41] We will be questioned about how we spent the number of years given to us. We will be asked about the blessings bestowed upon us and how we used them, including our eyes, tongue, ears, etc.

Praying on time, helping someone, visiting the sick, sympathizing with others, or even planting a tree are some good deeds that can make our route to *Jannah* easy. Just saying *Subhan'Allah* or doing the *dhikr* of *Subhan'Allahi wabihamdihi* adds an enormous number of good deeds to our account. For example, whoever says, '*Subhan'Allahi wabihamdihi*' one hundred times a day will be forgiven for all his sins, even if they were as much as the foam of the sea (Ṣaḥīḥ Bukhari). Whoever says *Subhan'Allah* one hundred times, a thousand good deeds are written for him, and a thousand evil deeds are wiped away from him (Ṣaḥīḥ Muslim). On the contrary, when our time is spent absentmindedly in committing sins (i.e., looking at *haram*, not praying, stealing people's rights, quarrelling, backbiting, and slandering) without even realizing, that leads to a waste of our entire lifetime. We must be mindful of our time and make sure that we do not spend it against the will of Allah ﷻ.

41. Both humans and animals exist on the planet. However, humans are given the *rooh*, the soul, which separates them from all other living beings. Humans also live much longer compared to most, if not all, living creatures.

Second question: How did we spend our youth?

In the later years of life, it is natural for an individual to feel drawn towards the remembrance of Allah ﷻ and take steps to acquire as many good deeds as possible. When the body is frail and the children have grown up, there is nothing else to do, and the person inevitably becomes more cognizant of the prayers and other religious pursuits to please Allah ﷻ. But senescence brings limitations. The older body needs a chair to pray and requires help from family members for physically demanding rituals, such as during *Hajj* and *Umrah*. The real test is when a person is young, and the energetic body can perform *ibādah* (worship) with concentration, such as fasting, giving dawah, waking up for *Tahajjud*, going for *Umrah*, and *Hajj* (if one is able to afford it), etc.

However, spending our youth according to the will of Allah ﷻ does not mean avoiding worldly activities. It is permissible to obtain an education, earn money, get married, travel, play sports, etc. We should balance our *dīn* with the *dunya* (world). It is essential to remember the limitations set by Allah ﷻ. We must spend our youth in gaining maximum good deeds such as praying on time, obtaining and spreading the knowledge of our *dīn*, doing the *dhikr* of Allah ﷻ, reciting the *Qur'an* daily, maintaining ties of kinship and being a means of benefitting others for the sake of Allah ﷻ. The key is to closely check and scrutinize our daily routine regularly. Are we living according to our *nafs* or as per the principles set by Allah ﷻ? The one who is obedient to the laws of the *Qur'an* and spends the time of youth remembering Allah ﷻ can accomplish the companionship of those who will be blessed with the shade of Allah's throne on the Day of Judgement. We must not take the time of youth for granted.

The third and fourth questions are interrelated: how did we earn our wealth and how did we spend it?

Having a good financial status is a blessing from Allah ﷻ. It is regarded as *khair* (goodness) at one point in the *Qur'an*.

يَسْـَٔلُوْنَكَ مَاذَا يُنْفِقُوْنَ ۗ قُلْ مَآ اَنْفَقْتُمْ مِّنْ خَيْرٍ فَلِلْوَالِدَيْنِ
وَالْاَقْرَبِيْنَ وَالْيَتٰمٰى وَالْمَسٰكِيْنِ وَابْنِ السَّبِيْلِ ۗ وَمَا تَفْعَلُوْا مِنْ
خَيْرٍ فَاِنَّ اللّٰهَ بِهٖ عَلِيْمٌ ﴿٢١٥﴾

They ask you as to what they should spend. Say: "Whatever good you spend should be for parents, kinsmen, orphans, the needy and the wayfarer; and whatever good you do, Allah is All-Aware of it."
(*al-Baqarah 2: 215*)

We earn money to fulfill our needs and to live comfortably. Allah ﷻ has fixed specific regulations and strategies for both employment and trading. Whether a Muslim is a labourer, a farmer, a trader, or an office employee, Allah ﷻ has set some rules we must abide by. For example, trade or business is allowed if there is no lying, or usury (interest) in it.

The Prophet ﷺ said, "The honest and trustworthy merchant will be with the Prophets, the truthful, and the martyrs." (Tirmidhī 1209).

Any dishonesty or fraudulent activity while trading may bring temporary profits, but at the expense of *Jannah, astaghfirullāh*. The same applies to situations if one is employed by an unlawful business, such as at a casino, or a place that involves the use of *riba* (interest) or deals with *haram* food and alcohol. One must also note that it is also forbidden for an employee to show disloyalty and lack of commitment when fulfilling his office duties. It includes taking unnecessary breaks, wasting time, or arriving late at work. All these frameworks become the provenance of *haram* income.[42] Whether there is a lot of workload or not, if you are required to be at your workplace for eight hours a day, then you must follow accordingly. It is a requisite for you to rightfully focus on the job, as the company pays you for this purpose. Disregarding these principles in this temporary world is easy, but such minor negligence can lead to *Jahannam*.

Narrated by *Abu Hurayrah* that the Prophet ﷺ said, "Certainly a time will come when people will not bother

---

42. Scholars have regarded employment disloyalties as equal to someone who does fraud in the trade. Allah ﷻ has used strict words in the *Qur'an* for such people, "*Woe to the curtailers, who, when they measure something to receive from people, take it in full, and when they measure or weigh something to give it to them, give less than due.*" (*al-Mutaffifin 83: 1-3*)

to know from where they earned their money, by lawful means or unlawful means." (Ṣaḥīḥ al Bukhari 2083)

Abu Hurayrah reported that the Prophet ﷺ said, "Allah ﷻ says: "O those who believe, eat of the good things that We gave you." The Prophet ﷺ then mentioned a person who travels widely, his hair disheveled and covered with dust. He lifts his hands towards the sky (and thus makes the supplication): "O Lord, O Lord," but it is not accepted because his diet is unlawful, his drink is unlawful, his clothes are unlawful, and his nourishment is unlawful. How can then his supplication be accepted?" (Ṣaḥīḥ Muslim 1015)

The second question regarding wealth is its expenditure. Our *dīn* gives us guidelines for this as well. Start with your household, where spending money on it is considered a charity.

The Prophet ﷺ once mentioned, "To leave your heirs rich is better than to leave them poor, begging from people. You would be rewarded, therefore, even for a morsel of food that you put your wife's mouth." (Ṣaḥīḥ Muslim 1628a)

Spending money on attaining comforts in daily life is permissible. However, if our intention is to show off, it becomes *haram*. It comes under *riyā* (ostentation) and *israaf* (extravagance). In the same way, spending your wealth on destructive activities such as gambling movies, and music is also prohibited. On the other hand, the wealth that is spent (according to our budget) on *sadaqah* relieves difficulties in this life and in the Hereafter *Insha'Allah.*

The Prophet ﷺ said: "A man giving a dirham as *sadaqah* (charity) during his life is better than giving one hundred dirhams as *sadaqah* (charity) at the moment of his death." (Sunan Abi Dawud 2866).

Fifth question: We were given knowledge, what did we do with it?

These days, we consider an Islamic scholar to be someone who has completed the course of *fiqh Hadith,* which consists of about eight years of training. However, the knowledge and comprehension mentioned in the question do not refer to any academic degree. It relates to recognising Allah ﷻ through His signs by thoughtfully observing Allah's creation and obtaining knowledge from it. Notice the cycle of nature, such as how the rain starts and how fruits grow on the trees. The knowledge of *dīn* is not limited to the information we obtain from books. It also includes educating yourself and your family on the basics of *farḍ* (mandatory acts of worship), *wājib* (highly recommended acts), and the *Sunnah.* This includes the basic understanding of the mandatory components in *wuḍū'* (ablution), the *Sunnah* of *ṣalāh,* and so on. It also includes grasping the fundamental concepts of marital issues, which unfortunately are not discussed in our society.

Enlightening others by giving *dawah* is also included in the rights of knowledge given to us by Allah ﷻ. *Dawah* means calling others to Islam and was the glorious mission of all the Prophets (peace be upon them all). The *ummah* will find success and happiness by following the *Qur'an* and *Sunnah*. Allah ﷻ has therefore commanded us to convey the message to all of mankind.

ادْعُ إِلَىٰ سَبِيلِ رَبِّكَ بِالْحِكْمَةِ وَالْمَوْعِظَةِ الْحَسَنَةِ وَجَادِلْهُم بِالَّتِي هِيَ أَحْسَنُ ۚ إِنَّ رَبَّكَ هُوَ أَعْلَمُ بِمَن ضَلَّ عَن سَبِيلِهِ وَهُوَ أَعْلَمُ بِالْمُهْتَدِينَ ﴿١٢٥﴾

Invite (mankind, O Muhammad) to the way of your Lord (i.e., Islam) with wisdom (i.e., with the Divine Revelation and the Qur'an) and fair preaching and argue with them in a way that is better. Truly, your Lord knows best who has gone astray from His path, and He is the Best Aware of those who are guided.
(*al-Nahl 16: 125*)

May Allah ﷻ help us answer all the five questions in the *Ākhirah, āmīn*.

Our Guidebook – The Qur'an

I recently returned from a short trip to Malta and Cyprus. Malta is a small European country with a growing population of Muslims. In the early 1900s, the area was chosen by the British to imprison Muslim scholars since it had no direct connection with a mainland. Some of the prominent scholars from South Asia were also incarcerated in Malta. Mawlana Mehmoodul Hasan (may Allah ﷻ grant him *Jannah*), a scholar at Darul Uloom,[43] was also among the captured prisoners. He was working on a task to unite the Muslim leaders of Afghanistan, Turkey and the Indian subcontinent. Unfortunately, he was arrested by the British and sent to a prison camp in Egypt and from there to Malta, where he was kept for three years. During his confinement, Mawlana was grateful to Allah ﷻ that his arrest was not for any offence or misdemeanour, but for a campaign done in the name of Allah ﷻ. The stories of his time in prison are narrated in the book written by one of his companions, Mawlana Syed Hussain Ahmad Madani.

Mawlana Mehmoodul Hasan completed the translation of the Holy Qur'an during his detention period in Malta, *Subhan'Allah*. When released, he returned to his homeland, the Indian subcontinent, and continued his tradition of giving lectures under a tree. One day, he

43. This Darul Uloom is the parent institution. Of its contemporary branch in Pakistan. The seminary was established in 1866, and to date remains one of the largest Islamic schools in the world.

recalled his time of imprisonment and said, "When I was in prison, I had time to reflect on the current condition of the Muslim world. I came to the conclusion that there are two main reasons behind the downfall of the Muslims. The first is turning away from the *Qur'an*, i.e., by not reciting it, understanding it, or following what is commanded in it. The second is the division amongst Muslims."

The first step in knowing the *Qur'an* is to recite it with the required *tajweed.* Unfortunately, we may hear people saying that reading translation is enough and that there is no requirement for the Arabic recitation. This argument comes from individuals who think of the Qur'an as any other ordinary book. The one who doesn't have a routine of Qur'an recitation would not desire to understand its translation and study the explanation of the Holy Book. The Qur'an is the book from the Creator of the Heavens and the Earth. As our Prophet ﷺ said in a *Hadith*:

Abdullah ibn Mas'ud reported that the Prophet ﷺ said, "Whoever recites a letter from the Book of Allah ﷻ, he will receive one good deed as ten good deeds like it. I do not say that *alif laam meem* is one letter, but rather *alif* is a letter, *laam* is a letter, and *meem* is a letter." (Tirmidhī 2910)

There are ten good deeds for every letter recitation of the Qur'an, and *alif, laam, and meem* are three letter that bring thirty good deeds into our basket. In prehistoric times, the recitation of the Qur'an was a part of the daily routine of Muslims, especially after the *Fajr* prayer. Discussions on the *tafsir* (exegesis) of the Qur'an and the analysis of *Ṣaḥīḥ Hadith* were a norm in these gatherings. Everyone in a Muslim family practised understanding the Qur'an. Islamic countries were known for their knowledge of deen, comprehension of *Fiqh*, and other bifurcations, such as calligraphy and material sciences.

Let's assume that one of your close friends sent a correspondence in a foreign language. You do not understand anything mentioned in the letter. However, you cannot throw it away or forget about it as it is a letter from your dear friend who loves you. You would be curious to know what message is being conveyed, so you would attempt to get the translation. The Qur'an is also a message from the one who created us and who wants the best for us. It stays on our bookshelves, and we may recite it occasionally. Beyond that, unfortunately, we are unconcerned to make an effort to understand its translation. We tend not to make time to read the annotations and *tafsir*.

As Mawlana Mehmoodul Haasan mentioned, there is division among the Muslims. Sadly, this is still relevant in today's era, as Muslims are divided into many groups. We have different sects, where everyone considers themselves as the guided ones and others as the deviant ones. Sectoral differences are unavoidable, and having different schools of thought is not forbidden. However, we surpass the limits and waste all our energy regarding the opposite sect as sinful. This division brings ignorance to society. As a result, we blindly imitate the lifestyle of non-believers and are impressed by their way of living. Today, it is not just limited to sectoral differences; there are multiple groups within the sect where people are busy trying to prove others wrong. The benefit of our division goes to the disbelievers who take advantage of our ignorance. History reiterates the predicament of this division. There are examples of the downfall of the Ottoman Empire and how the Arabs and Turks were segregated, and we lost a ruling empire of several centuries. The only way we can clear our differences is by following the *Sunnah* of our Prophet ﷺ, who never cursed anyone or used foul language. We must resolve our differences with the references to the Qur'an and authentic *Hadith.*

May Allah ﷻ guide us to follow His divine book, understand its meaning, and implement its teachings in our daily lives, *āmīn.*

The Contentment of Gratitude

Shaddad ibn Aws ﵁ was a companion of our Prophet ﷺ who also became the narrator of the famous *Hadith* on *sayyidul istighfar*. It is a *du'ā'* regarded by the Prophet ﷺ as one of the best supplications to ask for forgiveness.[44] One day, when the Prophet ﷺ was close to depart from this world, *Shaddad* was sitting closer to him. He was in deep grief thinking about the beloved Prophet ﷺ. He said, "O Prophet ﷺ, this world now feels worthless." The Prophet ﷺ replied, "Shaddad ibn Aws, you will see the conquest of *Shaam* (present day Syria) and *Bayt al-Maqdas* by the Muslims, and you will get to work there as well."[45] The Prophet ﷺ further added, "O Shaddad! If you see the people amassing gold and silver, then say these statements a lot:

44. Sayyidul Istighfar is considered as the master *dhikr* of *tawbah*. The Prophet ﷺ said, "The most superior way of asking forgiveness from Allah ﷻ is, "O Allah ﷻ, You are my Lord. None has the right to be worshipped but You. You created me and I am your slave, and I am faithful to my covenant and my promise as much as I can. I seek refuge with You from all the evil I have done. I acknowledge before You all the blessings You have bestowed upon me, and I confess to You all my sins. So, forgive me, for nobody can forgive sins except You." The Prophet ﷺ then added, "If somebody recites it during the day with firm faith in it, and dies on the same day before the evening, he will be from the people of Paradise; and if somebody recites it at night with firm faith in it, and dies before the morning, he will be from the people of Paradise." (Bukhari 6306)

45. It is reported that as predicted by the Prophet ﷺ, *Shaddad ibn Aws* witnessed the victories of Muslims and lived through the time of all four caliphs and has his resting place in Jerusalem.

أَللّٰهُمَّ إِنِّي أَسْأَلُكَ الثَّبَاتَ فِي الأَمْرِ، وَ الْعَزِيمَةَ عَلَى الرُّشْدِ،
وَأَسْأَلُكَمُوْجِبَاتِ رَحْمَتِكَ وَ عَزَائِمَ مَغْفِرَتِكَ، وَ أَسْأَلُكَ شُكْرَ
نِعْمَتِكَ، وَحُسْنَ عِبَادَتِكَ، وَأَسْأَلُكَ قَلْبًا سَلِيْمًا، وَ لِسَانًا صَادِقًا،
وَأَسْأَلُكَ مِنْ خَيْرِ مَا تَعْلَمُ، وَ أَعُوذُ بِكَ مِنْ شَرِّ مَا تَعْلَمُ،
وَأَسْتَغْفِرُكَ لِمَا تَعْلَمُ، إِنَّكَ أَنْتَ عَلَّامُ الْغُيُوبِ

"'O Allah ﷻ, verily I ask of You for the strength of perseverance of obedience on the *dīn*, and determination in practising the *dīn* and goodness. And I ask of You for that which obligates Your mercy and resolutions for Your forgiveness. And I ask of You for the capability to be thankful for Your blessings and to worship You in a correct and good way. And I ask of You for a heart which is purified in belief and free from desires and a truthful tongue. And I ask of You for the best of what You know, and I seek refuge with You from the evil of what You know, and I seek forgiveness for that which You know. Indeed, You are the One who knows the unseen."

The above *Hadith* highlights a crucial point. When people around us are occupied with worldly luxuries, we must direct our focus towards asking Allah ﷻ for perseverance by saying, "O Allah ﷻ, bless me with perseverance in performing good deeds, and perseverance to do them regardless of anyone distracting me or making fun of me and that I keep doing it to please you."

Generally, we find it easier to initiate a good deed. For example, we may feel energetic and motivated to begin praying extra *nafl* prayer or *dhikr* someday.

But after a point, repeating it every day becomes difficult, and eventually, we may stop doing it altogether. Sometimes, it is due to the busy schedule of our worldly matters, and other times, it is our *nafs* that makes it difficult for us.[46] This is why scholars instruct to make *du'ā'* and to ask Allah ﷻ to provide us with the courage to perform good deeds with consistency. Let's take with the example of water. Suppose a faucet pours the water over a rock with increased pressure. It may quickly wash over the surface of the rock and nothing else. However, if the same faucet drops only a drop of water at a time, the water strikes the rock underneath. A time will come when the water creates a dimple on the rock's surface, eventually penetrating it. That is the power of perseverance. A persistent drop of *'ibādah* can penetrate the rock of difficulties and make way for us in the *Ākhirah, insha'Allah.*

The second point in the *Hadith* is about the courage to perform a good deed. Frequently, we intend to do good but fail to execute it. Even though we understand it is a good deed, we do not feel drawn to act upon it. This is because we listen to our *nafs* and rely on fulfilling our interests. Consequently, we become a slave to our desires, rather than the slave of Allah ﷻ. Allah's slave is the one who is always ready to do good. The blessing of doing good also comes from Allah ﷻ, and that is why the Prophet ﷺ recommended to make *du'ā'* for it.

---

46. The temptations of our *nafs* often lead us away from voluntary acts of worship, convincing us that they are unnecessary.

The third virtue in the above *Hadith* about doing *shukr* for the blessings given to us by Allah ﷻ. Again, the moral strength for doing this comes from Allah ﷻ. As humans, we are the most ungrateful among all living beings on our planet. We have thousands of blessings showering upon us simultaneously; however, when we are afflicted with trials, we tend to focus only on the problem and become completely oblivious to the favours. Being grateful for the blessings and counting them also comes from Allah ﷻ. Therefore, we must make *du'ā'* for it. *Iblīs* and our *nafs* are our biggest enemies. *Iblīs*, the *Shaytan*, easily takes us towards ingratitude by making us focus only on the problems. That is why Allah ﷻ says in the Qur'an:

اِنَّ الْاِنْسَانَ لِرَبِّهٖ لَكَنُوْدٌ ﴿٦﴾ وَاِنَّهٗ عَلٰي ذٰلِكَ لَشَهِيْدٌ ﴿٧﴾

***Indeed, man is ungrateful to his Lord and indeed he is witness to that!* (*al-'Āadiyāt 100: 6-7*)**

In this *ayah*, Allah ﷻ is expressing anger that humans are ungrateful despite Allah ﷻ giving us countless blessings, including eyes that see, ears that hear and a heart that beats. Humans can talk, walk to different places and are provided with *rizq*. But instead of remembering the innumerable blessings, we focus on our problems.

رَبِّ اَوْزِعْنِيْٓ اَنْ اَشْكُرَ نِعْمَتَكَ الَّتِيْٓ اَنْعَمْتَ عَلَيَّ وَعَلٰي وَالِدَيَّ
وَاَنْ اَعْمَلَ صَالِحًا تَرْضٰىهُ وَاَدْخِلْنِيْ بِرَحْمَتِكَ فِيْ عِبَادِكَ
الصّٰلِحِيْنَ ﴿١٩﴾

***My Lord, enable me to be grateful for Your favour which You have bestowed upon me and upon my parents and to do righteousness of which You approve. And admit me by Your mercy into [the ranks of] Your righteous servants.* (*al-Naml 27: 19*)**

We have the example of Prophet Suleiman ﷺ who was bestowed with all the worldly blessings, yet he was grateful to Allah ﷻ. In the *ayah* above, Suleiman ﷺ asked for the blessing of being a grateful servant.

Mawlana Syed Asghar Hussain (may Allah ﷻ grant him *Jannah*) was an eminent scholar. Once, he was suffering from a high-grade fever. When my father, Mufti Muhammad Shafi, visited him, he was anxious to see Mawlana's deteriorating health. When asked how he was feeling, Mawlana replied, "*Alhamdulillah*, I am well. My eyes are working well, and my ears are working fine. I am able to talk. I am thankful to Allah ﷻ that I do not have such and such illness." He recollected the names of various diseases that he did not have. Mawlana Asghar Hussain completed his sentence by adding, "Yes, I have a mild fever. Please pray that Allah ﷻ gives me *shifa* from it." *Subhan'Allah*, such are the people of an elevated *īmān* who remember to show gratitude even when suffering from a fever. When we are blessed with the quality of *shukr*, we begin looking for the good in every situation. Being grateful to Allah ﷻ is a treasure, and our connection with Him strengthens when we practise it.[47]

---

47. Allah ﷻ has promised in the Qur'an, "*If you are grateful, I will give you more.*" (*Ibrahim 14: 7*)

قَالَ اَنْظِرْنِيْٓ اِلٰى يَوْمِ يُبْعَثُوْنَ ﴿١٤﴾

قَالَ اِنَّكَ مِنَ الْمُنْظَرِيْنَ ﴿١٥﴾

قَالَ فَبِمَآ اَغْوَيْتَنِيْ لَاَقْعُدَنَّ لَهُمْ صِرَاطَكَ الْمُسْتَقِيْمَ ﴿١٦﴾

ثُمَّ لَاٰتِيَنَّهُمْ مِّنْۢ بَيْنِ اَيْدِيْهِمْ وَمِنْ خَلْفِهِمْ وَعَنْ اَيْمَانِهِمْ وَعَنْ
شَمَاۤىِٕلِهِمْ ۗ وَلَا تَجِدُ اَكْثَرَهُمْ شٰكِرِيْنَ ﴿١٧﴾

Satan replied, "Give me respite till the day they shall be raised." Allah said, "You are granted respite." Satan said, "Since You have led me astray, I shall surely sit in ambush for them on Your straight path. Then I will come upon them from the front and the rear, and from their right and from their left. And You will not find most of them thankful."
(*al-A'raf* 7: *14-17*)

When *Iblīs* was thrown from the heavens, he said what is mentioned in the above *ayah*. This shows that the first attack of *Iblīs* is on gratitude, and the easiest way to fight him is by being eternally grateful to Allah ﷻ.

Once, I accompanied one of my teachers for dinner at a restaurant. The menu was extensive, and the food seemed appetizing. On seeing the dinner table, my teacher said: "Food is one of the biggest blessings by Allah ﷻ. There are five main blessings in it. First, imagine not having food and how hard it would be to settle a hungry stomach. Secondly, having delicious food is another blessing. Imagine having lots of food, but it's all rotten, bitter and tasteless. Thirdly, imagine having delicious food, but you are not hungry or allowed to eat it. Fourthly, imagine having delicious food; you are hungry, but the host is disrespectful while serving the meal. Surely, you would not enjoy having a meal after being humiliated. Finally, imagine having delicious food when hungry and being served respectfully, but suddenly, there is an emergency, such as the tragic news of someone's death. You would not want to eat and would lose your appetite, and if you do eat, the food will lose all its taste."[48]

There are innumerable blessings that accompany one plate of food. Moreover, imagine how the food is reaching you. Simple wheat bread was once a wheat crop somewhere in a land. It was then milled into wheat flour and mixed with water and other ingredients. This formed a dough, which was finally baked into bread. Imagine the fruit in your hand was once on a tree. It was transferred through numerous channels and finally reached your hand. Remember that the sustenance written for you will get you.

The fourth point in the *Hadith* is about *husna ibaadatik* and it refers to the beauty of the prayers, i.e., praying according to the *Sunnah* of Prophet ﷺ. The fourth point is interrelated with the fifth one which is about having a truthful tongue.

---

48. A beautiful reminder about the blessing of food. We must all recall these blessings at the time of eating, and also teach our youngsters about it.

Sidq, or truth, is to perform an *ʿibādah* correctly, with full concentration. *Ikhlāṣ* means sincerity, especially when submitting to Allah ﷻ. Because *sidq* and *ikhlāṣ* are interconnected, we must possess both when we perform our *ʿibādah*. Let's take the example of *ṣalāh*. When praying according to the *Sunnah*, it is *sidq* to pray how the Prophet ﷺ did, and *ikhlāṣ* is praying only for Allah ﷻ and not for showing to others. Performing an *ʿibādah* with *ikhlāṣ* but not according to *Sunnah* does not contain *sidq*. We should pray for a tongue that speaks the truth and is used according to the laws of Allah ﷻ.[49]

The sixth point is having a *qalban saleeman*, a heart full of prosperity. *Subhan'Allah*, the words of our Prophet ﷺ carry an in-depth significance. A person with a heart full of prosperity is one who thinks well of others and is involved in the *dhikr* of Allah ﷻ. This heart can appreciate righteousness. One of the omens that come from our sins is that our heart loses its potential to differentiate good from evil. A prosperous heart focuses on goodness and warns us against anything that takes us away from the *dhikr* of Allah ﷻ. That is why we should make *du'ā'* for it. May Allah ﷻ bless us with a prosperous heart.

The final point in the *Hadith* is about striving for *khuluqam mustaqeeman*, the morals that keep us on the right path. We must also ask for virtues known only to Allah ﷻ and missed by us in our supplications. We must ask for the goodness which is outside our understanding

---

49. A truthful tongue is free from backbiting, cursing and lying and it does not spread false rumours or slanders.

but is in the divine knowledge of Allah ﷻ Who knows what is best for us. Furthermore, we must not forget to ask Allah ﷻ to keep us away from evil wrongdoings (including the ones we are not aware of).

The above *du'ā'* is a treasure that our Prophet ﷺ asked *Shaddad ibn Aws* to keep instead of desiring worldly gold and silver. How do we get this treasure? One way is to memorize the *du'ā'*, and another way is to recall its meaning. This beautiful *du'ā'* has all the treasures we need in this temporary life to attain ease in our graves and the Hereafter.

Abu Huraira reported: The Messenger of Allah ﷺ said, "Take up good deeds only as much as you are able, for the best deeds are those done regularly, even if they are few." (Sunan Ibn Majah 4240)

Following the Sunnah

It is narrated by *Abu Huraira* that the Prophet ﷺ said, "All my followers will enter Paradise except those who refuse." They said, "O Allah's Messenger ﷺ! Who will refuse?" He said, "Whoever obeys me will enter Paradise, and whoever disobeys me is the one who refuses (to enter it)."(Ṣaḥīḥ al-Bukhari 7280)

As Muslims, we have been shown a path that takes us to the love of our Creator. It is the path that brings calmness to the mind and contentment to the soul, even when we are busy with worldly activities. We feel closer to Allah ﷻ and become one of His favourites just by following it. It is the path of the *Sunnah* of our Prophet ﷺ.

قُلْ اِنْ كُنْتُمْ تُحِبُّوْنَ اللّٰهَ فَاتَّبِعُوْنِيْ يُحْبِبْكُمُ اللّٰهُ

Say, "If you love Allah, then follow me (Muhammad), Allah will love you." (al-Imran 3: 31)

Allah ﷻ has given each one of us different temperaments and personalities that make up our *akhlāq* (morals character), and the one who had the best *akhlāq* was our beloved Prophet Muhammad ﷺ. The above *ayah* tells us that we can get closer to Allah ﷻ by following the lifestyle practises of the Prophet ﷺ. We have been blessed with a role model, and how beautiful it is, that the Creator of the heavens and the earth selected the best human and then directed us to follow him ﷺ. It is like gifting someone the best preparatory material for the final exam.

We are most beloved to Allah ﷻ when we follow the *Sunnah* of Allah's beloved human, our Prophet Muhammad ﷺ. For example, when waking up in the morning, say the morning *du'ā'* of our Prophet ﷺ:

اَلْحَمْدُ لِلّٰهِ الَّذِىْ أَحْيَانَا بَعْدَ مَا أَمَاتَنَا وَ إِلَيْهِ النُّشُوْرُ

***All praise is for Allah who gave us life after having taken it from us, and unto Him is the resurrection.* (*Ṣaḥīḥ al-Bukhari 6324*)**

When entering the bathroom, we must develop a habit of saying the following *du'ā'*:

أَللّٰهُمَّ إِنِّىْ أَعُوْذُبِکَ مِنَ الْخُبُثِ وَ الْخَبَائِثِ

***(In the name of Allah). "O Allah, I take refuge with you from all evil and evildoers."* (*Ṣaḥīḥ al-Bukhari 142*)**

Even though we are entering the bathroom, the *Sunnah* can still bring you closer to Allah ﷻ.[50]

---

50. *Shaykh* Taqi Usmani places significant emphasis on following the *Sunnah* supplications. His well-known work, "*Easy Good Deeds,*" also highlights his recommendations for memorizing and implementing Prophetic *du'ā'* in daily routines. *Sunnah* supplications are often repeated in his speeches, providing readers with valuable insights.

When following the *Sunnah*, our minds are directed so that they start revolving around the *dhikr* of Allah ﷻ. This means that an individual desires to build a stronger relationship with Allah ﷻ. It is an easy path, and we can start it today.

Our Prophet Muhammad ﷺ taught us every little detail we require for our daily routine. He taught us how to perform our duties, including worldly matters, such as, how to live a happy married life, friendships, trading, eating, drinking, sleeping, and even minor tasks like cutting nails. No area of life was left unguided. We have the attributes of his life, and this is why it is easy to follow the *Sunnah*, as our Prophet's ﷺ ways were the most natural and pure. He did everything in his life, from domestic chores, trading, and farming to leading the state.

لَقَدْ كَانَ لَكُمْ فِيْ رَسُوْلِ اللّٰهِ اُسْوَةٌ حَسَنَةٌ لِّمَنْ كَانَ يَرْجُوا اللّٰهَ
وَالْيَوْمَ الْاٰخِرَ وَذَكَرَ اللّٰهَ كَثِيْرًا ﴿٢١﴾

***There has certainly been for you in the Messenger of Allah an excellent pattern for anyone whose hope is in Allah and the Last Day and [who] remembers Allah often.* (*al-Ahzāb 33: 21*)**

We should study the books of *Sunnah*, reflect on how many of them we are following, and analyze which areas we need to put more effort into. Our entire *dīn* should be based on the Qur'an and *ittiba-e-sunnah* (following the *Sunnah*). Unfortunately, today, we have limited the practise of *Sunnah* to certain areas, such as during *ṣalāh*, *Umrah* and *Hajj*. But the fact is that the *Sunnah* is applicable to every area of our life, for all the people currently present and the ones coming after us. May Allah ﷻ help us follow the *Sunnah*.

وَمَآ اَرْسَلْنٰكَ اِلَّا رَحْمَةً لِّلْعٰلَمِيْنَ ﴿١٠٧﴾

And We have not sent you but as a mercy for all the worlds. (al-Anbiya 21: 107)

Abdullah bin Amr was one of the companions of the Prophet ﷺ who was a successful businessman. Because of trade, he knew the people of other communities, such as the Jews and Christians, and had also read the *Torah*. Once, someone asked him about the qualities of the Prophet ﷺ that are mentioned in the *Torah*. *Abdullah bin Amr* replied by reciting the verse:

'Verily, We have sent you (O Muhammad) as a witness, as someone who brings glad tidings, and as a warner' (*al-Fath 48: 8*) which is in the Qur'an appears in the Torah thus, "Verily, We have sent you (O Muhammad) as a witness, as a bringer of glad tidings, and as a warner and as a protector for the illiterates (the Arabs). You are my slave and My Apostle, and I have named you *Al-Mutawakkil* (one who depends upon Allah ﷻ). You are neither hard-hearted nor of fierce character, nor one who shouts in the markets. You do not return evil for evil, but excuse and forgive. Allah ﷻ will not take you unto Him till He guides through you a crocked (curved) nation on the right path by causing them to say:

"None has the right to be worshipped but Allah ﷻ." With such a statement, He will cause to open blind eyes, deaf ears and hardened hearts.' (Ṣaḥīḥ al-Bukhari 4838)

In the *ayah* mentioned in the above *hadith*, we notice that Allah ﷻ has mentioned, 'You are my slave' for the Prophet ﷺ. It means that although Prophethood is the highest level a human could achieve, being a slave of Allah ﷻ comes before being a Prophet. Similarly, when we say, *"I bear witness that there is none worthy of worship except Allah ﷻ, the One alone, without a partner, and I bear witness that Muhammad is His servant and Messenger,"* it means that the highest level for a human is to be the *abd* of Allah ﷻ. In English, the term *abd* has been translated as the slave or worshipper i.e., someone completely submerged in his duties. When someone is a servant, he is like an employee, with scheduled hours. He comes to work, and once the job is done, he is not under his employer. In contrast, a slave is always under the order of his master. He works continuously. It is not permissible for a slave to disregard his master. What level comes after slavery? Beyond slavery is the status of the *abd* of Allah ﷻ. *Abd* is the one who not only follows all the commands of his master but also worships his Master, Allah ﷻ. He follows whatever comes from the Divine Master without any condition. He remains content with any condition his Master puts him through.

How do we reach the level of such utmost devotion of an *abd*? First, by identifying whether our actions are pleasing Allah ﷻ or displeasing Him. Is there anything in our life that is not according to the rules of

Allah ﷻ? Second, staying content in whatever circumstances Allah ﷻ decides for us, thus accepting the divine decree. The one who was the best in *abdiyat* was our Prophet Muhammad ﷺ. When the Prophet ﷺ went to *Ta'if,* he was treated in the most inhumane way. Even in a situation when he felt extreme thirst, and his shoes overflowed with blood, he prayed, "Oh Allah ﷻ, as long as You are happy with me, it does not matter if they treat me with stones or give me pain. I am satisfied with Your divine decree."

Dhun'noon al-Misri, a Sufi scholar from Egypt once said, "Whatever happens in my life is never against my wishes." People were surprised after hearing this. They questioned how anyone can make such a claim because everyone's life has happiness and sorrows every once in a while. On hearing this, he replied, "This is because I have surrendered my will in the path of Allah's divine decree, and I stay contented with anything Allah ﷻ decides for me, be it hunger, satiety, sadness or happiness."[51]

Our Prophet Muhammad ﷺ was at the premier level of *abdiyat.* He laid an example for us that the path to true happiness and inner peace lies in the complete submission and utmost devotion of the slave. Other prophets also practised *abdiyat.* Suleiman عليه السلام ruled over the entire world, which not only included humans and

51. Shaykh Taqi Usmani eloquently incorporates the teachings of the pious predecessors in his lecture. Although it may initially appear unrelated, it ultimately ties in with the topic of discussion.

animals, but also *jinns*. Despite his powerful position, he lived as a slave of the Almighty.

Whether it is the throne given to Prophet Suleiman ﷺ or the sickness given to Prophet Ayyub ﷺ, all our prophets accepted the will of the Almighty Creator and lived as the *abd* of Allah ﷻ.[52] Of course, in difficult times, the term *abdiyat* indicates accepting the circumstance and asking Allah ﷻ to provide help in difficult situations. This is what our beloved Prophet Muhammad ﷺ taught us.

We are constantly thinking, and our *nafs* is always talking to us. Our aim is to guide it towards servitude and constantly remind ourselves that we the slaves of Allah ﷻ. A time will come when the light of *taqwa* will enter inside us. That is when life starts revolving around the remembrance of Allah ﷻ.

May Allah ﷻ make all of us His *abd*, *āmīn*.

---

52. Wealth and kingdom were a test for Suleiman ﷺ, and sickness and poverty were a test for Ayyub ﷺ. Through the stories of His prophets in the Qur'an, the Almighty tells us being in a state or difficulty is a tests for us.

Humanity

For centuries, when a student starts learning *a Hadith*, the first Hadith that is taught is called *Hadith* of *Rahma* (mercy), also known as *Hadith-ul-Musalsal bil Awwaliyyah.* It is as follows:

اَلرَّاحِمُوْنَ يَرْحَمُهُمُ الرَّحْمٰنُ

***Those who have mercy, The Rahman will have mercy on them.* (Musnad Ahmad)**

اِرْحَمُوْا مَنْ فِى الْأَرْضِ يَرْحَمْكُمْ مَنْ فِى السَّمَاءِ

***Have mercy on those who are on the earth and the one in the sky will have mercy on you.* (Musnad Ahmad)**

In the above *Hadith*, the Prophet ﷺ mentioned that whoever has mercy on others will also benefit from the mercy of Allah ﷻ. Having compassion for everyone includes the whole of humanity, irrespective of their level of *taqwa* (piety) or even faith. Everyone deserves mercy. The method of humanitarianism may be different, but there must be no repugnance towards any person or community. Hatred is for the *kufr* (disbelief and infidelity), not for the individual who is involved in it. Those involved in *kufr* are like people suffering from a disease. They deserve our sympathy and prayer for *hidāyah* (true guidance), and not our anger.

It is important to understand this concept as some of us are blessed and guided by Allah ﷻ because we pray *ṣalāh* on time, and observe fasting, and so on. However, we must be vigilant and not fall into the trap of *Shaytan*.[53] If the feeling of being more pious than others takes over, a person may begin to think, "I am the only one who is dutiful, everyone else is not religious and not doing the right things in life."

We do not know how the end of life will be like for us. The thought of being superior in religion drowns us in the ditch of sins. We are not aware who ranks higher than us in *īmān*. The internal affairs of the heart are known only to Allah ﷻ. Therefore, we should not look down upon anyone, even if we see someone sinning. Unfortunately, being devout is taken as the authority to look down upon others and be judgemental.[54]

There is an interesting story about a student and his shaykh. One day, the student said to his shaykh, "My dear shaykh, I saw you in my dream last night. Your hands had honey on them, and my hands had dirt."

---

53. For a practising Muslim, the trap of shaytan will be to make him feel proud of his *ʿibādah* and consider others as inferior to him.

54. Here, it is important to emphasize the importance of one's state at the end of their life, whether one dies as a believer or a disbeliever. There are stories where individuals who were pious throughout their lives died as disbelievers, while others who were disbelievers embraced Islam just minutes before their death. This serves as a reminder that the time of death is uncertain, and any moment may become our last one. We must seek protection from a bad end through Allah's grace.

The shaykh replied, "Yes, it is because I am a shaykh, and you waste your time in worldly matters." The student interrupted his shaykh and said, "Respected shaykh, I did not finish telling you the dream. In my dream, you had honey on your hand, and I had dirt, but you were making me savour the honey, and I was letting you eat the dirt on my hands." The interpretation of this dream is that the shaykh was teaching religious matters to his students, but he developed pride and considered them lower in rank.

We must never think of ourselves as superior to others. Scholars even went to the extent that we must not think of ourselves as superior to the disbelievers because anyone can be blessed with the jewel of *īmān* if Allah ﷻ wills. What matters is how we depart from this world.

Everyone in our world deserves empathy, either in the form of making *du'ā'* for them or giving them appropriate advice when needed. It is important to note that one must advise others at the right moment. Otherwise, it may lead to a negative outcome. Once, Hassan and Hussain raḍiyallāhu 'anhum, the grandsons of the Prophet ﷺ, were travelling. On their way, they noticed an elderly man performing *wuḍū'* incorrectly. To not show any disrespect to him, they remained silent. When the elderly man completed his wudu, Hassan رضي الله عنه approached him and politely asked, "Could you please help me in one matter? When I do my *wuḍū'*, I feel that I am not following the *Sunnah*. Would you see my *wuḍū'* and tell me if I'm doing it the right way?" The man agreed.

When Hassan ؓ performed *wuḍū'*, the elderly man realized his mistakes and learned the correct technique. This shows that Hassan ؓ used gentle mannerisms for his teaching.[55] This is how our ancestors were: neither harsh nor judgemental towards anyone. Unfortunately, it is a common practise in our society to publicly criticize others, as though Allah ﷻ has given us the right to reprimand them. The same matter can be explained privately in a respectful way. In this way, we can avoid feeling supremacy over others.

One time in Baghdad, an elderly scholar was travelling on a boat with his companions. There were young men on board with them who were enjoying their ride by playing musical instruments. On seeing the group of religious scholars, they started mocking the elderly scholar. The companions felt anguish and rage at the insults thrown at their teacher. They asked the scholar to curse the young men who were unkind to the one who followed the path of the Prophet ﷺ. The teacher raised his hands and prayed, "O Allah ﷻ, bless these young men with contentment in the *Ākhirah* just like how You blessed them with happiness in this world." The companions were astonished upon hearing the prayer. The teacher then explained, "My dear companions, if Allah ﷻ decides contentment for them in the *Ākhirah*, He will rectify their matters in this world too. What is our loss in this?" The

55. According to the sources, this story is from *Allama Kardari rahimahulla's Manaqibul Imam Al Azam*, vol.1 pg. 39.

scholar demonstrated a beautiful example of empathy. He wished good for everyone, just like our beloved Prophet ﷺ. In one *Hadith*, the Prophet ﷺ said:

"My example and the example of the people of my *ummah* is that of a man who lit a fire, and moths and other insects started falling into it. The man tries (his best) to prevent them, (from falling in the fire) but they overpowered him and rush to the fire." The Prophet ﷺ added, "Now, similarly, I prevent you from falling into the Fire, but you insist on falling into it." (Ṣaḥīḥ al-Bukhari 6483)

That was the level of empathy our beloved Prophet ﷺ had. As a result of his teachings, the attitude and character of the successive generations of Muslims became one of the leading causes of the propagation of Islam across the world. We must never forget that it is Allah ﷻ Who decides the jewel of *īmān*, for whom He likes. Maybe Allah ﷻ decrees someone's *hidāyah* through our kind disposition.

Ataullah Shah Bukhari (may Allah ﷻ grant him *Jannah*) was a renowned scholar of his time. He once went to a dinner with a company. While he was eating, he noticed a sweeper standing nearby watching him eat. He offered the sweeper to join them for dinner, but he was hesitant. Ataullah Bukhari insisted and made him sit in the gathering and even shared his plate with him. The young boy was so impressed with his gestures that he was eventually illuminated with the light of *īmān, subhan'Allah.*[56]

Our Prophet Muhammad ﷺ was sent as *Rehmatul lil Aalimeen* (Mercy for all worlds) for everyone on this planet, including humans, animals, birds and for everything else. As his *ummah*, we must develop the attribute of mercy. The first step is to have compassion for the creation of Allah ﷻ and it is only possible when enmity is replaced by sensitivity. One of the key factors in ameliorating resentment towards others is by making *du'ā'* for them. This is the way our Prophets used to pray for their people: by being kind and merciful to everyone.

May Allah ﷻ increase the spirit of compassion in society, *āmīn*.

56. It is narrated by *Sahl ibn Sa'd* that the Prophet ﷺ said to Ali رضي الله عنه, "By Allah ﷻ, if a single person is guided by Allah ﷻ through you, it will be better for you than a whole lot of red camels." (Riyad as-Salihin 1379) The herd of camels was considered a sign of great wealth in Arabia during those times.

Acquiring Knowledge

There are two types of *ilm* (knowledge): *ilm-e-zaahiri* (basic understanding of a subject) and *ilm-e-baatini* (an in-depth knowledge and grasp on the matter). Asking Allah ﷻ for knowledge is mentioned in the Qur'an.

رَّبِّ زِدْنِي عِلْمًا ﴿١١٤﴾

***O my Lord, increase me in knowledge.* (*Tā-Hā 20: 114*)**

Allah ﷻ asked His beloved Prophet ﷺ to ask for *ilm*. Our Prophet ﷺ was blessed with the most *ilm* among all. Despite this, he was asked to pray for an advancement in knowledge and an increase in understanding.

Ilm-e-zaahiri is to have a superficial understanding, for example, to understand the meaning of Qur'anic *ayah, Hadith, fiqh*, and so on. It includes what we read in the textbooks, such as the *ayah* and *Hadith* on the importance of the prayer, fasting, *zakat*, and other matters of the deen. The second branch of knowledge is *ilm-e-baatini* which is in respect to our connection with Allah ﷻ. Through this *ilm*, our mind is occupied with thinking about ways we can please Allah ﷻ. The best way to get to this level is to follow the *Sunnah* of Allah's beloved Prophet ﷺ. For instance, we learn a *Hadith* on helping others and easing someone's pain. We read and memorize it so we can spread this message to others. This is the *scholarly ilm i.e.*, the one that is often practised by our scholars. The other approach is to think about getting closer to Allah ﷻ by following the *Hadith* and taking encouragement from it, and hence bringing it into our daily routine is *ilm-e-baatini*. It means that the knowledge must not just stay in the mind but travels to the heart, and then unfolds into our actions. When we ask Allah ﷻ by saying *Rabbi Zidni Ilmaa*, we ask for both types of *ilm*, the external knowledge and the comprehensive one that inspires us to practise what we learn. *Alhamdulillah*, we are aware of the basic knowledge of *dīn*, but are we limited only to the external one? Or are we applying the knowledge in our daily life?

Rabbi Zidni Ilmaa also tells us that knowledge has an endless road. It is like an unquenchable thirst and an unsatisfied hunger. Allah ﷻ has told us through the Prophet ﷺ to ask for the advancement in our knowledge. Every human being must pray for it, regardless of age and gender. Take the example of someone who completes the exegesis of the Qur'an, studies the *Ṣaḥīḥ Hadith*, and then declares, "I have now completed all the education and have acquired all the knowledge." Such an individual is only fooling himself because knowledge is never-ending. Practising what we learn also has several stages and we advance in these stages as we go along. First is the basic technique of applying fundamental teachings of the *dīn* in our daily life matters, such as in our job, business, home, and also when performing *wuḍū'*, *ṣalāh*, fasting. Unfortunately, we are not even aware of these basics anymore. Today, if we ask about the mandatory acts of *wuḍū'* in our society, we may find that just a handful of people know the correct way. A common man who does *wuḍū'* daily may not be aware of the *Sunnah* and *farḍ* in *wuḍū'*. Likewise, the *Sunnah, wājib,* and *farḍ* during *ṣalāh* are not known to many.

Allah ﷻ has made it mandatory for us to understand the basic knowledge of our *dīn* (relevant to our daily life matters). Qur'anic *tajweed* is also missing in our society, although it is mandatory to study *tajweed* and recite the Book of Allah ﷻ correctly. Why is it being neglected? Because firstly, the basics are not known, and secondly, practising *ilm* is absent in the society. Not knowing the *farḍ* and *wājib* of the prayer means that we need to look for sources where we can study them. Allah ﷻ has blessed us with scholars who wrote books on the contents of *ṣalāh* which are available. If you don't know the *tajweed,* we have Qur'an teachers available to help us. If you find it difficult to find one locally, there are many videos available on the internet or Qur'an teachers who can teach you directly online.[57] And when the basic knowledge is acquired, our responsibility does not conclude there. Rather, we must continue to learn and bring it into our daily practise.

Imran al-Minqari reported, "I once said to Al-Hasan al-Baṣri, may Allah ﷻ be pleased with him, about something he claimed, "O Abu Sa'id, this is not as the jurists

---

57. As Muslims of the present time, we must be very fearful about our outcome because the knowledge of *dīn* is available to us at our fingertips. We will not be able to present any excuse to Allah ﷻ, unlike the people of the past who had to travel long distances in the desert to obtain the knowledge of *dīn*. Despite their difficulties, they were more aware of the matters of the *dīn*.

say." Al-Hasan said, "Woe to you! Do you consider only yourself as a jurist (*faqīh*) A true jurist is only an ascetic in the world, seeking of the Hereafter, insightful in the matter of his religion, and constant in the worship of his Lord." (Sunan al-Dārimī 30)

That is why when making the *du'ā' Rabbi Zidni Ilmaa*, we must remember the two types of *ilm*. Insha'Allah, as our knowledge increases, we will feel closer to Allah ﷻ. May Allah ﷻ provide us with both *ilm-e-zaahiri* and *ilm-e-baatini, āmīn.*

Index